America's Spiritual Utopias

The Quest for Heaven on Earth

David Yount

PRAEGER

Westport, Connecticut
London

Library of Congress Cataloging-in-Publication Data

Yount, David.
America's spiritual utopias : the quest for heaven on earth / David Yount.
    p. cm.
    Includes bibliographical references and index.
    ISBN: 978–0–313–35348–2 (alk. paper)
1. United States—Church history. 2. Utopias—Religious aspects—Christianity. 3. Utopias—
United States—History. 4. Utopian socialism—United States—History. I. Title.
BR517.Y69 2008
277.3—dc22   2007052917

British Library Cataloguing in Publication Data is available.

Library of Congress Catalog Card Number: 2007052917
ISBN: 978–0–313–35348–2

First published in 2008

Praeger Publishers, 88 Post Road West, Westport, CT 06881
An imprint of Greenwood Publishing Group, Inc.
www.praeger.com

Printed in the United States of America

The paper used in this book complies with the
Permanent Paper Standard issued by the National
Information Standards Organization (Z39.48–1984).

10 9 8 7 6 5 4 3 2 1

For Max Carter

Utopian

Then shall the wolf dwell with the lamb;
Nor shall the fierce devour the small.
As beasts and cattle calmly graze,
A little child shall lead them all.

Then enemies shall learn to love,
All creatures find their true accord;
The hope of peace shall be fulfilled,
For all the earth shall know the Lord.

Contents

Preface   xi

Introduction: The Perennial Quest   xiii

1. The Cloister: The Keys of the Kingdom   1

2. The Puritans: Building a City on a Hill   15

3. The Quakers: The Power of Friendly Persuasion   29

4. The Amish: Return to Paradise   43

5. The Shakers: Sharing Simple Gifts   57

6. The Mormons: To the Promised Land   71

7. The Oneida Community: Love One Another   83

8. The Salvation Army: Saving Body, Soul, and Spirit   97

9. The Catholic Worker Movement: The Virtue of Hospitality   113

10. Today's Utopias: A Place Just Right   127

Author's Notes and Acknowledgments   141

Timeline: Intentional Communities through the Ages   143

Notes   147

Bibliography   155

Index   159

The person who cannot live with himself
cannot live in community,
but the reverse is also true.

Dietrich Bonhoeffer

Preface

There are some 20,000 utopian communities in twenty-first-century America.[1] Most of them keep a low profile, welcoming new members without advertising for them. Nearly all are hidden from view—in rural America, in city slums, behind monastery walls. A majority of them are motivated by religious faith and seek to approximate heaven on earth. Some are startlingly successful.

The Hutterites, for example, are a mystery to most Americans, but there are 40,000 of them living like the first generation of Christians, pooling their wealth and living like an extended family. The Salvation Army, far from being a quaint group of Christmas bell-ringers, is a spiritual and practical movement that attracts over three million volunteers.

Our national history is utopian, wedded to the American Dream of the good life for all.[2] From the outset, settlers freed from the cynicism of the Old World welcomed the opportunity that beckoned in the New. The Puritans conceived of Massachusetts as the biblical city on a hill and light to the world. The Quakers made Pennsylvania a Holy Experiment. Like the Israelites before them, the Mormons trekked through a desert to create an empire of the spirit.

Even our failed utopias offer lessons. Sister Mildred, one of the last survivors of the once flourishing Shaker sect, lamented in her later years that "I don't want to be remembered as a piece of furniture."[3] As it is, Shakers are remembered less for their spiritual lifestyle than for the treasured chairs and implements they crafted.

Nevertheless, their uniquely American experiment in Christian communal living lasted longer than two centuries and attracted 6,000 lifelong members. They would still be with us were it not for their celibate lifestyle. Instead, the Shakers were challenged to maintain their numbers through conversion alone.

In 1967, *Life* magazine, profiling the survivors of the utopian experiment, quoted the aged Shaker Marguerite Frost:

Heaven is all around us. . . . You don't have to sprinkle yourself with water or get down on your knees to pray, or dance and sing like the early Shakers—religion is what you feel. It's what you are, not what you put on. . . . Christ is in all of us.[4]

As a result of the publicity, a flurry of requests was received for membership, mostly from men. But by then it was too late. Ninety-one-year-old Sister Lillian Phelps mourned: "We were not in a position to receive them. We can't teach them."[5]

The most inaccurate judgment to make of the Shakers would be to consider them quaint and impractical. They were neither. They were clearheaded and commercially successful. So are most of the subsequent attempts to create heaven on earth through community.

The very earliest Christians embraced a communal life of mutual concern, prompting pagans of the time to marvel, "See how they love one another!"[6] Contemporary spiritual communities in America enjoy the same motivation. To a disconnected secular society obsessed with unfettered freedom and acquisitiveness, these communities demonstrate the power of fellowship and sharing over individual isolation and narrow self-interest.

This is their story.

Introduction

The Perennial Quest

Our souls have sight of that immortal sea which brought us hither...
though nothing can bring back the hour of splendor in the grass, of glory
in the flower.

William Wordsworth[1]

While England's poet laureate was pining for a primordial Paradise forever lost to humankind, Americans were already creating new Edens in the New World. Although we have since faltered, we have never ceased the quest. As a people we are natural utopians.

During the Age of Reason, philosophers protested that this is already the best of all possible worlds, and we should make the most of it. Americans have always disagreed. The world falls far short of our aspirations and expectations. Our national history can be read as a persistent quest through common effort to make it better for all of us.

Of course, the utopian schemes contrived by dreamers in the Old World were not precisely mirrored in the New. Contrary to myths cherished by later immigrants to our shores, our streets were not paved with gold.

Still, the original dreams were never discarded but merely transformed by practicality, and they merged into the American Dream of the good life for all. That spirit of possibility persists in America, and our character remains utopian to this day. From the outset, settlers newly freed from the restrictions of the Old World welcomed the opportunity that beckoned in the New but realized that the frontier could not be pushed back without common cause.

Of necessity, the earliest Americans cast their lot with one another to convert a wilderness into a safe haven. Lamentably, Americans today are so mobile that many of us never become part of a community. Even if he expressed it clumsily, Yogi Berra understood why people still need other people. "If you don't go to somebody's funeral," he predicted, "they won't come to yours."[2]

SOCIETY AND SANITY

Utopians motivated by religious faith depict heaven itself as a society and argue that any earthly approximation must be conceived as an extended and interdependent family. In *Genesis* the Creator affirmed that it is not good for man to be alone. Utopians agree that *homo sapiens* is not a solitary species, but one that needs society to keep its sanity.

Most of the successful utopian enterprises in America have been prompted by religious faith. They aim to contrive earthly societies that approximate the biblical Eden, where man and woman were innocent, at peace with God, nature, and their fellow creatures, free from hurt and hunger, responsible for and nurtured by their companions.

Those utopian ventures inspired by the Christian faith have aimed at emulating the very earliest community of believers, of whom it was written:

There was complete agreement of heart and soul. Not one of them claimed any of his possessions as his own, but everything was common property. . . . A wonderful spirit of generosity pervaded the whole fellowship. Indeed, there was not a single person in need among them. For those who owned land or property would sell them and bring the proceeds of the sales and place them at the apostles' feet. They would distribute to each one if he were in need.[3]

Outsiders marveled how the members of that community cared for one another. Their radical rejection of personal property was probably prompted by their belief in the imminent end of the world. But, free of that millennial expectation, faith-based utopian communities in America still favor common property (or at least generous sharing) as a guarantee of solidarity and freedom from want.

Utopians share a belief in the essential goodness of human nature and the possibility of perfection. The glue that binds them is commitment, not coercion. Members of utopian communities are persuaded that their individual interests coincide with the values of the group, and that their personal growth is nurtured by others. Many Americans still share this faith but no longer act on it. We might be happier if we did.

In a sense, utopian communities represent a reversion to tribal society. But, whereas members of true tribes are physically related to one another, intentional communities must rely on common values, not blood, to attract like-minded strangers to share their lives and work. Utopia is a return to tribalism with this important difference: it is radically egalitarian. In an intentional community, it is not enough to be nondiscriminatory as to the sex, race, religion, education, sexual orientation, or even ability of its members. Everyone is not only treated equally but is appreciated as the equal of every other member. And they are all equally responsible for one another.

Fortunately, the rest of us need not escape to a commune, ashram, or monastery to enjoy utopian values. They can be borrowed and injected into everyday living in our families and workplaces.

HIDDEN HAVENS

Christian utopians in America enjoy a magnificent history. From the outset, the American continent was a great testing ground for community builders. The Puritans built their Eden in Massachusetts, the Quakers in Pennsylvania, the Mormons in Utah, and the Shakers in many states. But those were only among the most prominent attempts to build heaven on earth in the New World. Following the Great Awakening of our nation's colonial period, utopian communities proliferated across the nation in the nineteenth century—Oneida, New Harmony, Brook Farm, Fruitlands, Amana, Bishop Hill, and many hundreds more. Of the earliest communities, the Amish, Mennonites, and Hutterites remain the most visible in contemporary America.

But most utopian communities are invisible to us because we do not know where to look for them. Hundreds of monasteries across America perpetuate a utopian model of the common life that has persisted since the sixth century AD. The Salvation Army enrolls 3.3 million Americans as volunteers to pursue its utopian vision of service to the needy, but they are visible to most of us only during the holiday season. Catholic Worker "houses of hospitality" are caring communities for the homeless and dispossessed across America, but they are located in city slums and ghettoes that we tend to bypass.

Every human community, however primitive, is a contrivance that aims to balance people's self-centeredness with their need for companionship and community. The utopian seeks more: to make people better than they are so they will be better for one another. In the utopian view, just as the universe is ordered by natural principles, so can society be ordered and people made perfect.

Considering the odds against manufacturing perfect people in a flawless society, utopians are routinely dismissed as impractical dreamers. But they have even harsher critics. Sigmund Freud argued that utopians represented not an evolution to a higher stage of human development but a regression to a more primitive state.[4]

The father of psychoanalysis believed that mature human development requires the separation of egos, and the independence of the individual from the group. Freud especially deplored the wedding of utopian ideals to religious faith, considering it a ploy to sustain childhood dependency.

In point of fact, there is no room for childishness in utopia, where everyone must pull his own load for the benefit of all. The American journalist Charles Nordhoff, having visited many utopian communities in the nineteenth century, concluded:

Men cannot play at (community). It is not amateur work. It requires patience, submission; self-sacrifice often in little matters where self-sacrifice is peculiarly irksome. . . . "Bear ye one another's burdens" might well be written over the gates of every commune.[5]

VALUE AND COMMITMENT

But why would anyone freely choose to take lessons from communities that are often short on privacy, independent action, and material comfort, and long on labor and discipline? Emotional and material security plus the company of one's fellows are surely incentives, but they fall short of explaining why anyone would contribute his property and vow lifetime allegiance to a community as so many utopians did and still do.

Every utopian community must solve similar problems in order to secure and nourish its members' commitment. There may be no trash to dispose of in heaven, but in every heaven-on-earth someone must take out the garbage. Members must devise ways to get work done without reverting to coercion. They must make decisions that meet with everyone's satisfaction, build solidarity while avoiding cliques, select and initiate new members, ensure a degree of privacy and autonomy, and nurture shared values.

Those of us who live in the larger society manage differently. We work for strangers or companies to earn our living, pay for our private home or apartment and one or two cars, focus on our own needs and those of our families, choose our friends freely, and demand exclusivity in our affections. We are possessive in our love. We hire others to take our trash.

Utopians find something seriously missing in such a life. The journalist Charles Dana reminisced about Brook Farm, a colony founded by Transcendentalists in nineteenth-century Massachusetts, and suggested the missing ingredients:

The healthy mixture of manual and intellectual labor, the kindly and unaffected social relations, the absence of everything like assumption or servility, the amusements, the discussions, the ideal and poetical atmosphere which gave a charm to life, all these combined to create a picture towards which the mind turns back as to something distant and beautiful, and not elsewhere met with the routine of this world.[6]

Wordsworth might have identified it as the moment of splendor in the grass and glory in the flower.

True utopian communities seek permanence through life-long commitment. Successful communes are not only based on sharing, but also demand sacrifice, abstinence, investment, labor, some sort of ritual, plus some means for mutual criticism of members. At first blush, these mechanisms for commitment seem to drain utopia of any appeal. In fact, they are challenges that strengthen the members' commitment to one another. Cost is, after all, a measure of value. The monk's vows of poverty, chastity, and obedience bind him closely to his community precisely because the more he invests of himself, the more he is inclined to value the community, and expect it to reciprocate his allegiance.

ECSTASY AND ESCAPISM

Utopians challenge the general society, many finding it to be crass, impersonal, inequitable, materialistic, and amoral. But utopia also has its critics, some of whom complain that communes choose contentment over vitality and challenge. On the whole, the evidence does not support their contempt. For example, while studying the mental health of contemporary Hutterites (who number some 40,000 utopians in North America), Joseph Eaton and Robert Weil not only found much less neuroticism than in the general American population, but also more caring within the community for members in mental anguish.[7]

Moreover, the creation and sustaining of an intentional community commands the energy of its members. Far from being boring, it is an ongoing and uncertain adventure against substantial odds. The long-lived utopias of past and present had to survive not only natural disasters, but migrations, the creation of new communities, and the hostility and persecution of their neighbors.

Utopian communities tend to favor the simple life as their approximation of heaven on earth. Still, every successful community must strike a balance between austerity and ecstasy. The monk abandons personal possessions, autonomy, and marriage, but he joins with his brothers in song for hours each day. The celibate Shakers toiled in silence every day, but danced ecstatically at night.

Against their critics, utopians insist they are activists, not escapists, and that the rest of us can profit from their successes. The Salvation Army and the Catholic Worker movement serve unmet needs of the greater society. Even the traditional monastery serves our society by praying for it and providing a safe haven for harried Americans seeking temporary solitude and peace. The Quakers provide material relief and reconciliation to victims of war and natural disasters. Many contemporary faith-based communities care for prisoners, immigrants, addicts, the poor, and the conflicted. Utopians have always been a force for peace in the larger society.

To create a truly caring society, Americans would require a common faith. In its absence, our spiritual utopians, professing faith in the best in human nature, offer us practical lessons about the pursuit of happiness through community that the rest of us can incorporate in our lives.

Those lessons emerge in the following profiles of actual American utopian communities and movements, past and present. I have favored the most successful, long-lived, and effective models, most of them faith-based. The attempt to build heaven on earth is more likely to succeed if one happens to believe there is a real heaven to emulate. Many of these utopian enterprises still exist and are growing. More are being created. Despite differing visions of heaven on earth, each pursues the best of all possible worlds.

Chapter 1

The Cloister:
The Keys of the Kingdom

A monastery is at once a microcosm and a paradise...(The monks) were poor, they had nothing, and therefore they were free and possessed everything.

Thomas Merton[1]

The monastic life is at once the most ancient, purest, and most successful of experiments aimed at creating the best of all possible worlds through community.

"How good and pleasant it is for brethren to dwell together in unity," proclaims the Scripture.[2] Monks and nuns renounce personal property and take vows of poverty, chastity, and obedience to speed their search for personal perfection and mutual fulfillment.

Each member concedes the quest is impossible to achieve on one's own, so all freely choose to be dependent on one another and responsible to the community.

Relatively few Americans are candidates for the cloistered life, but we can learn from unrelated men and women who acknowledge that all people are brothers and sisters. To that end, many cloistered communities sponsor secular "Third Orders" for like-minded people in the world. Their members gather regularly in localities across America to support one another and serve those in need.

For the past twenty years, my wife and I have lived contentedly in an exurban community that is built around a meandering artificial lake and an eighteen-hole golf course. Because it is planned, enclosed, free of commerce, patrolled by a private security force, and governed by detailed covenants and bylaws, our community is as artificial as the lake and country club it surrounds.

Although our enclave is not gated, some of our neighbors feel locked-in by the restrictions. To thrive in a place like this, one must appreciate community rules as conditions for contentment. Permission must be sought for any additions or alterations to homes, even a change in paint color or planting a hedge. What an individual resident may consider an improvement to his property, the community is likely to consider an aggravation. For example, satellite dishes are taboo; so are clothes-lines and basketball hoops. Dogs must be leashed and picked-up after. Parking is regulated, trucks are not allowed, boats are restricted to electric motors. Years ago, a resident who replaced his standard-issue black mailbox with a blue one was successfully sued by the community. Predictably, plastic pink flamingos are an endangered species on local lawns.

Most of the residents are content with the tradeoffs, preferring the freedom of living in a beautiful, secure place to residing in neighborhoods where individualism means anything goes. Not in their wildest public relations dreams did the community's developers aspire for it to be an earthly paradise. Nevertheless, it shares this characteristic with every utopian enterprise: the cost of community is the restriction of individual liberty. But truly successful communities manage to contrive rules that actually enhance the individual initiative of their members.

In an age that worships self-esteem, privacy, and personal rights, and aspires to working and entertaining oneself in solitude, it is tempting to forget the creator's wisdom that it is not good for people to be alone. Henry David Thoreau, America's most celebrated exponent of the solitary life, nevertheless kept chairs for guests at his Walden Pond retreat and after several seasons abandoned solitude altogether to return to the society. He explained, "I left the woods for as good a reason as I went there....I had several more lives to live, and could not spend any more time for that one."[3]

The biblical Eden was not a solitary paradise but a compact society that included a man and a woman, the beasts of air, water, and fields, and the creator himself, who walked with the man and woman in the garden. There they were self-sufficient and content until the problem with the apple arose. Subsequent history can be read as a series of attempts to re-create that paradise. Whatever else heaven is, it is surely a society with the creator at its heart. So it is of no wonder that utopians who seek to build heaven on earth are motivated by faith.

THE CLOISTERED LIFE

Rome fell to the barbarians in 410 and was sacked again in AD 455. The last emperor was deposed in 476. With the fall of the empire, civilization disintegrated. By then, Rome was no longer pagan but Christian. No matter: religious faith alone could not protect the citizenry from barbarism. As society imploded, many devout Christians fled the dangerous cities in anticipation of the biblical apocalypse.

Some fled society altogether, becoming hermits. But most sought to build protected, self-sustaining communities wherein they might emulate the primitive Christian community, in which all property was shared and marriage was set aside in anticipation of the second coming of Christ. Believers in any age protest their love for God, but life in close community is its test, because in that crucible one must love one's brothers as well.

These self-contained, self-governing communities of celibate men and women pursued a simple and devout life. Ironically, as Europe descended into the Dark Ages, the austere monasteries became repositories of ancient civilization and learning, and the simple monks and nuns were the most educated men and women in Christendom.

Worldly sophistication was never their intention. A man or woman entered a monastic community to seek perfection—not selfishly, but for God, who made man and woman in his image—and for Jesus, who enjoined his followers to "be perfect as my Heavenly Father is perfect."[4]

Any account of utopian communities of faith in America must begin with the monastic community, because every subsequent attempt to construct heaven on earth is a variation on the monastic model. Revealingly, there is nothing antiquated or foreign about life in such communities. Monasteries are everywhere in the United States, and life in the cloister has changed little since Saint Benedict imposed a rule for practical common living on his fellow monks early in the sixth century.

Monastic communities no longer protect themselves from marauders by high walls such as they built in the ninth century to discourage Viking invaders. Many contemporary American monasteries are light, airy structures utterly unrelated to the gothic or romanesque. (In Utah, the Trappist community lives and worships in World War II surplus quonset huts while raising cattle for a living.) The two monasteries I know best are St. Anselm's Abbey in the heart of the Nation's Capital, where the

Benedictine monks support themselves by operating a prestigious prep school, and Holy Cross Abbey in rural Virginia, whose Trappists live by farming and commercial baking.

I dropped out of college briefly in my senior year to taste monastic life at Conception Abbey outside St. Joseph, Missouri, and I have visited communities of enclosed nuns in Rome and in Connecticut. Most, but not all, Christian monasteries in the United States are Roman Catholic. But even communities that draw their inspiration from Islam or Buddhism follow a traditional monastic model.

To be sure, family life in America is a species of the common life, with rules, expectations, and responsibilities—some explicit, others implicit—that bind the household and contribute to the mutual satisfaction of husband, wife, and children. The monastic community is yet another species—a voluntary family of unrelated men or women, bound by a common quest, as well as by celibacy, common property, obedience to authority, and life-long attachment. When he left his community, the "wandering monk" of tradition ceased being a monk at all.

THE COMMON QUEST

Few monks consider themselves or their common life to be utopian, because monastic life is, by contemporary standards, austere. But the cloister is not intended to be a pleasure garden. Rather, it provides a setting and regimen that enables the monk or nun to seek his or her true self. When the celebrated professor Carl Van Doren encountered his former student, the Trappist monk Thomas Merton, after many years, he remarked that Merton was little changed. Merton agreed explaining that the whole point of monastic life is to become more oneself—the person God had in mind in his original design. Monastic life aims (like a snake shedding its skin) at dispensing with one's false self to discover the true.

Another reason why monks are uncomfortable with being identified as utopians is because they consider utopians to be dreamers, whereas members of monastic communities are tough-minded realists. Examples of monastic life existed long before Benedict, and monastic communities are as vital in the twenty-first century as they were in the Age of Faith. There is every indication that they will continue to offer a practical alternative lifestyle that many men and women vastly prefer to the lives the rest of us pursue in the world of competitive commerce. Of this the monk is certain: ordinary life in the world, no matter how affluent, leaves much to be desired. Sacrificing the ordinary to pursue the extraordinary is a worthy adventure.

A monk, incidentally, does not necessarily aspire to be a priest, a personal status that could be superfluous to the needs of the community. Those needs are to be economically self-sustaining and allow sufficient time each day for the members to worship and study, as well as work. Celibacy is simply taken for granted as a condition for a common life that allows each individual the freedom to focus his or her life on the quest for God.

Living in community requires sharing; the so-called vow of "poverty" obscures the fact that the monk has everything he needs, but very little that is strictly personal property. Obedience is required not by arbitrary superiors, but to elected authorities and sensible rules. The vow of stability is not unlike the marriage vow: it means living in the chosen monastic family until death calls one to the celestial community.

THE RHYTHM OF THE CLOISTERED LIFE

If that vow sounds like self-imprisonment, Peter Levi would agree with you. The Oxford don and former Jesuit acknowledges:

At any visitor's first entry into a monastery, time seems to stand still. If one spends a week in one or a month, a different scale and pattern of time imposes itself, which at first one resists as if one were in prison. When this new time-scale is accepted, it soaks into one's bones and penetrates one's mind. It has nothing to do with death or eternity, but it involves a tranquil, unhurried, absolutely dominating rhythm...the greatest difference between the monastic life and any other.[5]

Levi remarks on the sameness monks achieve: "a silence of the spirit, a childish innocence, and apparently meaningless goodness. They become like good children by playing at being good."[6] Old monks, he notes, "perch more lightly on the globe than the rest of us" who put our abilities and superiorities on display. The monk is expected to assist (and not to impede) his brothers in the common life, but ultimately his only judge is his creator.

Monastic life is simple, and monks take a vow of poverty. But monasteries themselves are not necessarily poor. Indeed, the growing wealth of monasteries throughout the Age of Faith prompted chronic series of reforms aimed at restoring the simple life within the cloister.

The irony is that in the course of embracing poverty, the monasteries became rich. From the outset the cloister, far from closing its gates to the community outside its walls, welcomed the weary traveler, the poor, the sick, and the orphan. To the landless peasant, it provided work in its own fields. Monks educated children and provided medical attention. Because they were such worthy charities, monasteries attracted the legacies of wealthy Christians, who took seriously the Savior's warning that it is easier for a camel to pass through the eye of a needle than for a rich man to inherit eternal life.

It seemed to be a good bargain. Bequeath your wealth to the monks; in return they would pray for your salvation. After all, they prayed all day every day and well into the night—arguably much more prayer than they needed to ensure their own eternal reward.

Over time, however, wealth tended to corrupt monastic life. Rather than working for their own subsistence, the monks hired servants and laborers and life became comfortable. Moreover, female monasteries became the dumping grounds for the cast-off wives, mistresses, and unmarried daughters of aristocrats. Younger sons, prevented by the law of primogeniture from inheriting their fathers' land, entered the cloister not for the love of God, but out of desperation.

On the whole, reforms restored the simple life of the cloister, but over time the accumulated wealth of the monasteries both annoyed and attracted the secular rulers. When Henry VIII broke with the pope of Rome and proclaimed himself the Defender of the Faith, he began in 1536 to confiscate the wealth of England's monasteries, pension off the monks, and reduce their abbeys and priories to rubble. In the mid-seventeenth century, Oliver Cromwell and the Puritans completed the destruction. After 1789, across the Channel, the anticlerical hostility of the French Revolution forced European monasticism to decline. But beginning in the nineteenth century, America welcomed the monks with their farms and schools, and monasticism has flourished here ever since, attracting our native sons and daughters to the cloister.[7]

There is no "made in the USA" model for the cloister. When, on the eve of America's entry into World War II, the young Thomas Merton entered Kentucky's Gethsemani Abbey, his experience proved to be timeless. The monks at Gethsemani kept the traditional hours of worship and labor. Even the Abbey's architecture was reminiscent of medieval Europe. Trappists chanted in Latin to God but kept silent among themselves, so there was not even the sound of English conversation to remind Merton that he was in twentieth-century America. Moreover, the sixth-century rule of St. Benedict, with only minor revisions, governed the life of the community.

SAINT BENEDICT

Benedict of Nursia (ca 480–547) is the patron saint of Europe and the patriarch of Western monasticism. He was arguably the most influential Christian in the seven centuries that separated Augustine of Hippo from

Francis of Assisi and Thomas Aquinas. Benedict was literally the creator of the cloistered life as we know it, and his *Rule* remains the basis for the common life to this day. A devout but practical genius, he was a master of both human psychology and community management.

The founder of Western monasticism was born to affluent parents and raised in the ancient Sabine town of Nursia. In early adolescence, he was sent to Rome to receive a liberal education. Although officially Christian, the empire was besieged by pagan tribes and Arian heretics. According to *Butler's Lives of the Saints*:

The civilized world seemed during the closing years of the fifth century to be rapidly lapsing into barbarism: the church was rent by schisms, town and country were desolated by war and pillage, shameful sins were rampant among Christians as well as heathens, and it was noted that there was not a sovereign or a ruler who was not an atheist, a pagan, or a heretic.[8]

The young scholar's fellow-students imitated the vices of their elders. Fearing moral contamination, Benedict fled Rome to become a hermit in Subiaco, a rocky wilderness some 30 miles from the city. There he met a monk, Romanus, who clothed the young man in sheepskin and led him to a cave in the mountain. Benedict made it his solitary home for three years, unknown to anyone except Romanus, who daily lowered bread to him in a basket.

Absorbed in prayer, the young hermit lost all sense of time. When shepherds discovered the cave, they mistook the young hermit for a wild beast, because he was clothed in animal skins and lived exposed to the elements. Through no initiative of his own, Benedict attracted a group of fellow solitaries who pleaded with him to form a community and be their abbot. He reluctantly agreed, only to have the group attempt to poison him for his strictness.

Over time, Benedict established near Rome a dozen monasteries of twelve monks each. But when he attracted the envy of local clergy, he abandoned these fragile communities to found the great and enduring abbey of Monte Cassino, some 80 miles south of Rome.

Fourteen centuries later, it would be the site of one of the most brutal battles of World War II.

"NOTHING HARSH, NOTHING BURDENSOME"

For his fellow monks, Benedict composed (in his words) "a little rule for beginners, nothing harsh, nothing burdensome,"[9] that covered every aspect of life in the cloister, from electing the abbot as superior, to specifying psalms for daily prayer, corrections for faults, proper clothing, and acceptable amounts of food and drink. A year-long trial was required before an applicant could join the community permanently. If a monk left after taking his vows, he might apply for reinstatement in the community as many as three times.

In Benedict's reckoning, the monastery was a school to teach the service of God. The *Rule* begins impressively:

Listen carefully, my son, to the master's instructions, and attend to them with the ear of your heart. This is advice from a father who loves you; welcome it, and faithfully put it into practice. The labor of obedience will bring you back to him from whom you have drifted through the sloth of disobedience.[10]

The *Rule* recognizes that the individual monk's quest is both supported and tested by life in community. Any solitary seeker is prone to eccentricity and tempted to fanaticism. Moreover, he must furnish his own needs. By contrast, the monk in community is obliged to support his brothers, who share their bounty with him. By providing equally for the needs of the individual and the community, Benedict created a life that is (in Thomas Moore's words) "profoundly contemplative and thoroughly communal."

The monastic rule is an instrument for shaping a particular kind of life for which a person has deep and genuine desire. It is a tough life in certain ways—the rule can be harsh—but it is also in its own way liberating. It frees a person from the unspoken rules of the society at large and offers an alternative.[11]

Moore, a practicing psychotherapist who lived for twelve years as a monk, acknowledges that monastic rules can feed masochistic tendencies in some men and women, giving rise to anger, resentment, and depression. But in his experience "people living under the monastic rule generally have a good sense of humor and a lusty sense of life."[12] As a practical virtue humility rests squarely on a true estimation of oneself. Life in a permanent community effectively smoothes the rough edges of one's personality.

More than most people, monks appreciate life's absurdities, not least their own. In the cloister a gentle, self-deprecating sense of humor is more appropriate than the armor of righteousness.

A monastic community is based on holding property in common—being assured of one's necessities while claiming nothing as exclusively one's own. Every utopian experiment at least flirts with the notion of common property, whereas individualism focuses on acquiring personal property. Monks have their needs met without being personally responsible for getting and holding a job, making money, achieving raises and promotions, incurring debts, and paying bills. The monk is content to shed those personal anxieties in order to focus on his life-long quest.

In the cloister, celibacy is accepted not as a denial of sexuality, but as a rejection of possessiveness and exclusivity. Embracing the unmarried state is yet another way of dispensing with the burden of personal property in order to be free and wholehearted. Nor is obedience in the cloister intended to be burdensome, but rather to liberate the individual from the constant necessity of making decisions about what to do next. The word "obedience" in Latin literally means "to hear"—to listen to guidance for one's own benefit. The monk listens not only to the abbot and the rule, but to the needs of others.

HUMILITY AND CONTEMPLATION

"Your way of acting should be different from the world's way," Benedict told his monks. "Never give a hollow greeting of peace or turn away when someone needs your love....Speak the truth with heart and tongue."[13] Sincerity and mutual concern are essential for a healthy common life.

Humility, far from self-abnegation, is a lighthearted affirmation of one's limitations. The alternative, Moore notes, is "to set ourselves up for a lifetime of trying not to make mistakes and denying our faults." In devoting himself to a lifetime pursuit of perfection, the monk exemplifies what G.K. Chesterton said of all worthy quests: "Anything worth doing is worth doing badly."[14] Benedict proposes twelve steps to humility, whereby

the monk will quickly arrive at that perfect love of God which casts out fear. Through this love, all that he once performed with dread, he will now begin to observe without effort, as though naturally, from habit, no longer out of fear... but out of love....[15]

Revealingly, there is no mention of mysticism from Benedict—no prescriptive discipline for grasping divinity in some ecstatic experience, no experiential payoff this side of eternity. The saint's idealism for his monks is utterly practical, laying out a way of life that supports the individual pursuit of perfection for Christ's sake. Key to Benedict's pragmatism was to fix the monk's attention not on an invisible and ineffable God, but on his incarnation in Jesus, who lived as a man and demonstrated the quality of human perfection.

Benedict did not expect the abbot to style himself as a chief executive officer, running his community like a corporation, but "to amend faults and safeguard love" and "to arrange everything that the strong have something to yearn for and the weak have nothing to run from." His aim was "that in all things God may be glorified."[16]

Toward that end, the true work of the monk is to sing God's praises in concert eight times each day. Each morning before sunrise the community chants, "Lord, open my lips, and my mouth will proclaim your praise." Before retiring at the conclusion of a long day they sing, "May the all-powerful Lord grant us a restful night and a peaceful death."[17]

Does God need all this praise? Clearly not, but Jesus nevertheless implored his followers to "pray without ceasing,"[18] because prayer reflects the human need for God and connects with him. Some monasteries sing the Divine Office so beautifully that they market commercial recordings of their chant. My experience is that monks do not have better voices than anyone else, and there are as many who are tone-deaf as in the general population beyond the cloister. So God must be satisfied with the quality of what is offered to him.

The Divine Office is composed principally of the Psalms. Plain chant is just that—plain and largely repetitive—admirably suited for men or women who are not enchanted with the sound of their own voices, many of whom cannot read music.

THE MONASTIC DAY

Thomas Moore recalls his days in the cloister when

I rose at 5:15 A.M. to a knock on my door and a Latin greeting from a confrere. "*Ave Maria*," Hail Mary, he would say in a muffled voice on the other side of the door, breaking into my dreams. "*Gratia plena*," Full of Grace, was my reply, although it was often said with more growl than grace.[19]

Because its routines are so habitual, the cloister marks time by bells, not clocks. It is unusual to see a monk or nun with a wristwatch. Their only appointments are for prayer, reading, work, meals, and sleep, and their schedule seldom alters. Silence dominates, and there is no haste in the daily routine. Nevertheless, there are fixed intervals for each activity. No one tarries at meals, labor, or even reading.

Work is a necessity but is typically not laborious, because a community of monks aims only to be self-sufficient, and the monks' needs are not great. Today, monasteries rely less on agriculture and more on simple manufacture—bakery goods, jellies, and even books. Many monasteries operate schools within their confines, from prep schools to colleges. Benedict was intensely practical:

If there are artisans in the monastery, let them work at their arts with all humility....This principle pertains to all tasks in the monastery: when they need help, let it be given them, and when they have nothing to do, they should do what they are told.[20]

In the cloister, duties tend to rotate among the members, and no monk is above being charged with the most unattractive tasks. All utopian communities require that someone take out the trash; better that everyone take his or her turn. The two most distasteful tasks I have accomplished in my life were imposed during my seminary career: cleaning the grease traps in the community kitchen, and cleaning the carcasses of freshly slaughtered poultry. But I had plenty of company.

In community everyone pulls his weight. There are no servants and masters; everyone is a servant. Benedict insisted that work is not just a necessity but a virtue, wherein a man or woman shares in God's creativity.

A portion of each monk's day is devoted to study—*lectio divina* or spiritual reading. Prayer is not conceived as a one-sided conversation with God as listener. He must also be listened to for his revelation. Contemplative reading opens not only the mind but also the heart, revealing God's presence. The monk reads, meditates on the text, rests in the sense of God's nearness, then resolves to alter his life according to his improved understanding of his calling and quest.

In Benedict's time, there were few books for individual reading, so a monk read aloud at meals from a common text. To this day, it is still common for monks to eat in silence while listening to the word of God.

Benedict was not fussy about prescribing food and drink. He provided that two kinds of cooked foods be served at each meal in case a monk found one of them distasteful, plus fruit and vegetables, bread, and as much as half a bottle of wine a day, but no red meat. He considered two meals a day to be sufficient; modern communities make provision for three.

FAULTS IN THE FABRIC

Thomas Moore recalls the practice of "culpa" in his monastery, a public confession of faults to the entire community. Every close utopian community maintains discipline by making some provision for confession or fault-finding. Without them, irritations fester and hostilities grow. Just as husband and wife are advised by St. Paul not to go to bed angry, members of a close community must resolve their conflicts by telling the truth to one another, no matter how unpleasant.

Benedict was patient but firm in correction:

If a brother is found to be stubborn or disobedient or proud, if he grumbles or in any way despises the holy rule and defies the orders of his seniors, he should be warned twice privately by the seniors, in accord with our Lord's injunction. If he does not amend, he must be rebuked publicly in the presence of everyone. But if even then he does not reform, let him be excommunicated, provided that he understands the nature of his punishment.[21]

Even if separated from the community, the prodigal could apply to return and be accepted again into the monastic family.

Thomas Merton was echoing Benedict when he described the monastery as a school—"a school in which we learn from God how to be happy." All schools require discipline, and the best rule is internal. "God," Merton wrote, "must cleanse our souls of the lies that are in them."

Penances and humiliations serve to remind us of what we are and who God is—that we may get sick of the sight of ourselves and turn to Him; and in the end, we will find Him in ourselves, in our own purified natures which have become the mirror of His tremendous Goodness and of His endless love.[22]

HOSPITALITY

In the aftermath of World War II, Merton published an account of his young life. Before entering his monastery in Kentucky, he led an aimless and worldly life. After his death, it emerged that he had fathered a child while a student at Oxford. Both mother and child were presumed to have died in the Blitz.

Merton's book, *The Seven Storey Mountain,* was the third largest selling nonfiction title of 1948, going on to sell millions of copies in America alone and to be translated into sixteen languages. Ironically, it never made *The New York Times'* bestseller list, because the newspaper had a rule against including religious titles.

Merton's account of his wayward youth, his conversion to Catholicism, and entry into the cloister was more than a publishing sensation. It prompted thousands of veterans returning from the violence of war to seek the peace of the cloister. With that influx came a renascence of American monastic life.

Whereas many utopian communities distance themselves defensively from the greater society outside, the cloister has always welcomed the visitor. From the outset monasteries have offered accommodations and meals to the traveler and to those who seek sanctuary from the anxieties of everyday life in the world.

Benedict himself looked upon every guest as Christ in disguise, quoting Jesus: "I was a stranger and you welcomed me."[23] In his rule, the saint charged the abbot and community to wash the hands and feet of the weary guest. "Great care and concern are to be shown in receiving poor people and pilgrims," he decreed, "because in them more particularly Christ is received..."[24] Even the desert fathers before Benedict's time were so hospitable to strangers that they interrupted their prayers and fasts to welcome them.

My wife and I help to support the guest house of Holy Cross Abbey in Berryville, Virginia, which is always filled and has a lengthy waiting list of men and women who seek a few days of silence and simplicity. The monks accept guests of all faiths and none; the question of faith is never asked, and no bill is rendered for the hospitality offered—the monks making do with donations their guests can afford. Except for dispensing with the tradition of foot washing, they offer each stranger full welcome. In return for offering hospitality, Benedict told his monks to ask each stranger for his or her blessing.

Although few Americans are prepared to embrace the monastic life altogether, its utopian appeal is palpable and perennial. "It's a sweet life," a aged monk assured author Kathleen Norris.[25] She, like many other admirers of the cloister, mimics St. Benedict's rule in her busy, married life.

If the cloister is intended to be heaven on earth, does it follow that heaven will be like the cloister? In the Christian view, heaven is a permanent community with God as its focus and love as its rule. It is a place of happy sharing, security, and contentment without ambition or exclusivity. In these respects, the cloister is surely a pattern for eternity and a model for people of faith to anticipate eternity by building a heavenly society this side of paradise.

As a compact society for celibate men and women, the cloister cannot serve as the model for the greater society of family and commerce. How to construct a heaven on earth for everyone? The Puritans believed they had found a way in the New World.

Chapter 2

The Puritans:
Building a City on a Hill

We doubt not but God will be with us, and if God be with us, who can be against us?

Francis Higginson[1]

"The eyes of all are upon us,"[2] proclaimed the earliest Americans as they strived to create heaven on earth in the New World.

Motivated by religion, they believed that their destiny rested on their faith and that Providence would favor their community if they would be responsible to God and to one another.

They were at once skeptical about human nature, yet confident that by mutual assistance the faithful can rise above our natures, draw down grace, and fashion the best of all possible worlds.

The Puritans offer the cautionary lesson that intolerance ultimately destroys fellowship. Nevertheless, their example inspired their successors to create the lasting experiment in community that is the United States.

On November 11, 1620, a small group of English religious dissidents landed on Cape Cod and founded the Plymouth colony. The pilgrims had no charter, but all of the forty-one adults who disembarked from the Mayflower signed a compact that has since been celebrated as the introduction of democracy to America. In truth, the Mayflower compact was a one-sided arrangement that for forty years ensured tight control by a handful of founders led by William Bradford, who became the colony's first governor. During that first winter, half of the pilgrims died of disease and the elements.

A decade later, a well-financed group of Puritans, equipped with a royal charter and operating under the auspices of the Massachusetts Bay Company, sailed from England to form the communities of Salem, Boston, Charlestown, Dorchester, Roxbury, and Watertown—each centered on a covenanted church. Unlike the pilgrims, the Puritans protested that they had not separated from the Church of England, but were only adapting it to the New World.

In fact, they had a vision for America that sharply contrasted with both the established church and the Presbyterian ambitions of English Puritans. The New England Puritans dispensed with liturgy and hierarchy in favor of righteous living within local congregations, which became the focus of community life. Although dissenters themselves, they created a theocracy that did not tolerate dissent. In the next decade, more than 20,000 Puritans made the voyage from England to the Bay Colony, bringing tools, clothing, cattle, and eating utensils.

The first wave of settlers occupied themselves on their long voyage to America by listening to sermons. On the deck of the flagship *Arbella,* John Winthrop, their future governor, gave voice to the spiritual and secular aspirations of the Puritan utopia:

Thus stands the cause between God and us:

we are entered into covenant with Him for this work; we have taken out a commission...We must consider that we shall be as a city upon a hill, the eyes of all people are upon us. So that if we deal falsely with our God in this work we have undertaken, and so cause Him to withdraw His present help from us, we shall be made a story and a by-word through the world...[3]

Winthrop rallied the Puritans:

Therefore, let us choose life, that we, and our seed, may live; by obeying His voice and cleaving to Him, for He is our life and our prosperity.[4]

THE NEW ZION IN THE WILDERNESS

Unlike their European counterparts, the New England Puritans were unconcerned with theological disputation. Instead, they invested their energy in practical Christianity, applying the gospel to the formation of a righteous society in the New World. In 1637, the Massachusetts General Court prohibited anyone from settling in the colony who had not first proved his religious orthodoxy to the secular magistrates. Those citizens who wandered from orthodoxy were simply excommunicated and banished from the colony—a luxury that England, with its spectrum of competing faiths, could not effectively indulge.

Anyone who persisted in preaching a variation on the Puritan gospel was punished. Quakers were executed. The preacher John Cotton justified religious intolerance in the colony, insisting that a dissenter "is not persecuted for cause of conscience, but for sinning against his own conscience."[5]

Theoretically, there was a distinction between church and state in the colony, but effectively they were the same. To sin against the former was an offence against the latter. The Puritans held that there should be no intermediary church authority between the local congregation and God himself. Only those settlers who could make, in John Cotton's words, "a declaration of their experience of a work of grace"[6] could be members. Today we would characterize this sense of election as a born-again experience, the certainty of having been chosen and saved by God. Although the church was not meant to govern politically, only the elect could vote and rule in the Commonwealth, so it came down to the same thing. Biblical law ruled both church and state.

True to their Calvinist heritage, the New England Puritans believed human nature to be corrupt, but that God by covenant imputed righteousness to his elect, who were persuaded of their election by their experience of grace, and proved it by righteous living. Ironically, it was the Puritans' very pessimism about human nature that restrained them from thinking of themselves as utopians. In fact, they were radical utopian planners determined to build a practical heaven on earth. The Puritan spirit, if not in its strict Massachusetts form, dominated fully 85 percent of all churches in the original thirteen colonies and accounts for the persistent sense of manifest destiny in America to this day.

A PRACTICAL DOGMATISM

Historian Daniel J. Boorstin believes that their dogmatism actually liberated the early Puritans to concentrate on community-building, law enforcing, and fighting the Indian menace. "Had they spent as much of their energy in debating with each other as did their English contemporaries," he argues, "they might have lacked the single-mindedness needed to overcome the dark, unpredictable perils of a wilderness."[7]

The New England meeting house was modeled not on European church buildings but on a synagogue—a simple unadorned room without an altar, in which the pulpit stood prominent and the sermon was intended to instruct the community in its duties to God and one another. In the absence of a central church authority, the individual congregations nevertheless maintained a common quest and a way of living.

Congregationalism made do without intermediaries between the covenanted community of the elect and the God to whom they were responsible. There were neither priests nor ordinations, but only godly men called by the group to minister to them. The Puritans were steeped in the Bible but relied on scripture less for their laws than for their sense of mission, comparing themselves to the Israelites called out of bondage to make a godly nation in the wilderness.

They preferred precedents to creeds and institutions to codes. In practice, they closely followed the English example of appealing to custom rather than legislative fiat. When, in 1646, the General Court of Massachusetts was attacked for making church membership the criteria for secular citizenship in the colony, the Puritans pleaded their Englishness and placed the blame on their lack of trained lawyers. "There can be no just cause to blame a poor colony (being unfurnished of lawyers and statesmen) that in eighteen years hath produced no more, nor better rules for a good and settled government,"[8] the court pleaded in 1648.

Despite their claim of fidelity to the laws of the mother country, the Massachusetts Puritans were inclined to regard sins as crimes. To those offenses punishable by death, they added idolatry, blasphemy, man-stealing, adultery with a married woman, perjury aimed at securing another's death, the cursing of a parent by a child over the age of sixteen, and being a "rebellious son." Third offenses for burglary and highway robbery also merited the death penalty, contrary to English precedent.

In 1662, responding to increased criticism and the waning of fervor in second generation Puritans, the colony reluctantly created a new class of church membership for descendants of the original "saints" who could not demonstrate their forbears' overwhelming experience of election. Ordinary baptized, moral, orthodox persons could hereafter share in the privileges of church membership save for the taking of communion. By this time, England itself officially tolerated faiths other than the established church and demanded that the New England Puritans follow suit. In 1691, the original Pilgrim community of Plymouth was annexed to Massachusetts Bay.

STRICT VIRTUE

What we are inclined to view as Puritan vices, they took as virtues. Their authoritarianism was appreciated as a love of truth and dedication to duty.

Their very rigidity in doctrine afforded them the confidence to be flexible in application. There was a spirit of community in the Massachusetts Bay Colony which exceeded that in the other colonies. The very spirit that motivated the Puritans to report on their neighbors' deviations from morality prompted them to be equally solicitous about their neighbors' needs. Not less than monks, the Puritans valued labor as worship of the Creator. Their disdain for idleness and luxury and their inclination to save were admirably suited to the prodigious work of conquering a frontier.

Unlike monks, however, the Puritans did not freely choose poverty. True to their Calvinist roots, they looked to success in the world as a sign of God's personal favor, and a reward for their virtue. Predictably, over time, commercial success and general affluence prompted an erosion of personal piety if not morality. By the end of the seventeenth century, it was clear that Massachusetts was not the city upon a hill its founders had hoped it to be. Continuing problems with the Indians were attributed by preachers to God's judgment on the community. Fear became the handmaiden of superstition when witchcraft appeared to unleash demonic forces as God's own wrath. The witchcraft trials and hangings took place in Salem in 1692.

H. L. Mencken dismissed Puritanism as "the haunting fear that some-one, somewhere, may be happy."[9] Nathaniel Hawthorne's *The Scarlet Letter* is probably the prism through which subsequent generations in America have viewed the Puritan character—guilt-ridden, joyless, fanatical, dogmatic, prudish, antiliberal, and totalitarian. Can we forget poor Hester Prynne, Hawthorne's saintly adultress, impregnated by a hypocritical Puritan minister and forced to wear the letter "A" in shame? The fire-and-brimstone sermons of Cotton Mather appear to contemporary Americans to epitomize the Puritans. In fact, by the time Mather was in his prime, Puritanism had moderated its strictness, and the fiery preacher was trying to resurrect hell and damnation in their imaginations.

SIMPLE PLEASURES

Truth be told, there were happy Puritans who rejoiced in more than personal rectitude. Taverns were common in Puritan towns. Families on relief were provided not only food but also beer, cider, and even hard liquor at town expense. So, too, were volunteer laborers on community projects. Samuel Eliot Morrison paints a picture of early Boston that is anything but dour:

The ordinary weekday scene in Boston of the 1650s was active and colorful enough to suit a Dutch painter. Holland, France, Spain, and Portugal coming hither for trade, shipping going on gallantly, taverns doing a roaring trade with foreign sailors and native citizens, boys and girls sporting up and down the streets, between houses gay with the fresh color of new wood and the red-painted trim; the high tide lapping into almost every backyard and garden; and Beacon Hill towering over all.[10]

The Puritan preacher Samuel Willard acknowledged that our lives on earth should have "sometimes their ecstacies" and a preoccupation with eternity ought not to preclude bringing the earthly "wilderness to blossom."[11] Moderate pleasures, Joshua Moody preached, kept people from pursuing extreme ones. Oscar Wilde once quipped that Englishmen of his time believed themselves to be moral when they were only uncomfortable. For all their vaunted sobriety, American Puritans never held that actions were sinful simply because they gave pleasure.

Historian Bruce C. Daniels acknowledges that Puritan piety combined devotion with a strict moral code, but they were

people with sex drives, appetites, a sense of humor, and an appreciation of the need for pleasure in everyday life. "Sincerity," "consistency," "decency," "moderation"—these were the words attached to the Puritans' attitudes toward leisure, recreation, and morality...[12]

Morrison agrees that the Puritans enjoyed "durable satisfactions."[13] Sex within marriage was sanctioned by Scripture, refreshed body and soul, squandered neither time nor money, and was at least potentially productive. As a true son of the Reformation, John Cotton considered monastic celibacy an abomination. "God was of another mind," he wrote, than to believe in "the excellence of virginity."[14]

CIVIL LIBERTY AND LEARNING

On July 3, 1645, Governor John Winthrop addressed the Massachusetts General Court on the subject of human freedom. Natural liberty, he said, "is common to man with beasts—a liberty to evil as well as to good." It must be restrained by "all the ordinances of God"; otherwise man may become more beastly than others of God's creatures. Civil liberty, by contrast, gives man the freedom to do "only that which is good, just, and honest," he insisted. "This liberty you are to stand for, with the hazard of your lives, if need be."[15]

It fell to the Puritan leaders to distinguish what behavior was civilized and what beastly. In fact, there was remarkable conformity to shared values. Puritans rejected some leisure activities on purely practical grounds—football because it was violent, tennis because of its association with aristocrats, and some card games because they were an enticement to gambling. From the outset music lightened the otherwise austere worship services, and secular music became popular after the first few generations.

Dancing was something else. John Cotton consulted Scripture and found the dance permissible "lending to the praise of God,"[16] but was persuaded that social dancing fanned sexual desire. In the first Puritan generations, there was no mixed-sex dancing. When a dancing school opened in Boston in 1684, Increase Mather persuaded officials to prosecute, calling mixed dancing "vile, infamous, and abominable."[17] But sixteen years later his son, Cotton, reluctantly accepted public dancing, which was by then common across the colony.

One matter on which Puritans fully agreed was that literacy supported civilized behavior. The sooner human nature could be exposed to the rules of the good society, as revealed in the Bible, the better. So schools flourished. Boston had a school in 1635, Charlestown the next year, Dorchester three years later. Most were at least partly supported by taxes. In 1642, the Commonwealth of Massachusetts ordered parents and masters of apprentices to ensure that the colony's children were instructed in reading, religion, and law-abiding. Five years later, it required every settlement of at least fifty households to hire someone to teach reading and writing.

Larger settlements were to teach Latin as well to prepare youth for the university. Boston Latin School became the first secondary school in America, taking its students at the age of seven to study Latin initially, then Greek and Hebrew, as well as to cultivate "humane learning and good literature." Many of the early Puritan preparatory schools remain in operation to this day.

The quest for learning was fierce. Within a year of the Puritans' arrival in America, the Massachusetts General Court appropriated 400 pounds "towards a school or college." Two years later, when John Harvard died, he left his library and a legacy of 800 pounds for the institution that continues to bear his name. Originally, Harvard was principally a seminary, training men for the ministry. It accepted only those applicants who could read, write, and speak Latin in both prose and verse, and knew their Greek nouns and verbs.

The 4-year regimen for the bachelor of arts degree included grammar, rhetoric, logic, arithmetic, geometry, astronomy, ethics, ancient history, Greek, and Hebrew. A master of arts degree demanded three more years' study at Harvard. When the college expanded its curriculum to include the study of John Locke and Isaac Newton, a group of its alumni clergy broke away in 1701 to found Yale University in hopes of restoring Puritan tradition.

LIFE IN THE PURITAN VILLAGE

Historian Bruce C. Daniels acknowledges that "few if any societies in western Christendom achieved or aspired to as great a degree of cohesion as Puritan New England did."[18] It was in marked contrast with England and the Continent, where education and economic distinctions separated classes, townsfolk rarely mixed with the peasantry, and few except the affluent had contact with the clergy or a stake in government.

Puritan life in America, by contrast, was designed to be seamless. Politicians, ministers, craftsmen, magistrates, and farmers knew one another and were even interchangeable. Religious services were held in English, not Latin, the Bible was read in every home, and the plain meeting house symbolized the lack of distinction between religion and everyday living. The vaunted town meetings that continue to this day in New England villages are a tribute to the Puritan legacy of viewing life whole and making practical decisions with one's neighbors about the quality of community living.

The Puritans provided for their poor and needy; everyone was a member of a moral community. There were no separate holidays in the Puritan calendar, for fear that it would make other days of the year less holy. The medieval church calendar was abandoned by the first New England generation.

Because the Puritan villages were at some distance from one another, each asserted a practical autonomy. Often only the tacit approval of the Massachusetts General Court was sufficient for local decisions to be valid. It was, effectively, self-government by amateurs who had everything at stake in making the right decisions for themselves and their neighbors. The Puritan leaders' initial requirement that settlers build their houses within a half mile of the meeting house or local magistrate reflected the founders' wish for a cohesive society. It was repealed in 1640 as unrealistic and unenforceable.

The experience of Sudbury, Massachusetts, illustrates the pressures placed on community as its residents toiled to earn a living. Sudbury was a small interior town whose citizens raised cattle and farmed on common land, sharing their harvest with one another. By the early 1650s, needing more land, they applied to the General Court for an additional tract. But the locals could not agree on how it should be put to use. One faction wanted an equal portion for each farmer as private property. Older residents pressed to limit the number of cattle grazing on the town meadow. The town split over the matter of private land and livestock, with one faction moving away altogether to found Marlborough.

All utopian ventures confront the issue of personal property. For the Puritans, so long as there was sharing and provision for the poor, personal property was merely a sign of one's industry and God's favor. But in a wilderness, who was to decide how much land one could demand as one's own?

In Boston by 1634, the citizenry demanded an immediate and equal division of all available land. Governor Winthrop, fearing that the parceling of land would also divide the community, argued that more Puritan settlers would soon arrive in the colony and need homesteads. If they were forced to settle at great distances, they would lose the benefit of community altogether. Moreover, he argued, no one should own more land than he can farm himself.

Winthrop and his followers lost the argument. Existing land in Boston was divided among the current residents, while common lands were set aside for newcomers. But as early as the 1640s, there was already a shortage of plots for immigrants or additional acreage for established settlers. Across the Commonwealth, the problem of property was compounded when first-generation Puritans resisted dividing their farms among their sons. In Andover, for example, more than four of every five second-generation sons remained dependent on their fathers and lived in the community for their entire lives.

THE INEVITABILITY OF DECLINE

Puritan virtue suited the first generations in Massachusetts, who had a wilderness to conquer and a living to carve out. By contrast, in Anglican Virginia, planters fast became New World aristocrats, able to farm great plantations with the assistance of slaves. There a more comfortable and genteel lifestyle prevailed than in ascetic New England.

Vigor, hardship, and isolation are the conditions that Samuel Eliot Morison sees as supporting the Puritan quest. As we shall see in subsequent attempts to create heaven on earth in America, adversity is the unwitting ally of utopians. So long as there is hardship, ideal enterprises appear to be worth the effort and attract the strong in the quest. It is not an exaggeration to argue that Puritanism in America was a victim of its own success.

Puritan thrift and labor soon produced prosperity, and with it acquisitiveness and comfort. Harvard historian Bernard Bailyn notes that "the soul of the merchant was constantly exposed to sin by virtue of his control of goods necessary to other people."[19] Puritan ethics accepted profit as evidence of diligence in business. Profitability, in short, was virtuous, so long as it did not reflect avarice.

Recognizing the potential problem, the early Puritans preached that no one should exact more than a "just price." John Cotton explained: "A man may not sell above the current price, i.e., such a price as is usual in the time and place, and as another (who knows the worth of the commodity) would give for it, if he had occasion to use it...." But Cotton acknowledged that when a commodity is scarce, "there men may raise the price; for now it is a hand of God upon the commodity, and not the person."[20]

Of course, even honest merchants and farmers prospered. Moreover, contrary to the old Catholic prohibition of charging interest on loans, it was a fact of mercantile life and capitalism that money begat money. The early Puritans did not consider loans to be pure charity; they were to be repaid in full by the borrower. But John Cotton, quoting the authority of Exodus and Leviticus, insisted that "no increase...be taken of a poor brother or neighbor for anything lent unto him."[21]

Since the merchants themselves were required to borrow at interest for their inventory, they felt hard-pressed not to charge interest on consumer debts. The Reverend John White worried as well over the payment of just wages to workers with no productive property of their own. He argued that "the common good...is not furthered by such as draw only from one another and consequently live by the sweat of other men's brows, producing nothing themselves by their own endeavors."[22]

Robert Keayne, a London merchant tailor, arrived in Boston in 1635, was received into the church, made a freeman of the corporation, and quickly achieved prominence in local affairs. He proceeded to sell goods imported from England for whatever price he could get. In 1639, both church and state accused him of "taking above six-pence in the shilling profit; in some, above eight-pence; and in some small things, above two for one." Keayne was denounced in court and fined 200 pounds. In turn, the church treated him as a sinner, although he had been regular in attendance at worship and even kept notes on sermons for later study.

Never, he pleaded, had he indulged in "an idle, lazy, or dronish life" or afforded himself "many spare hours to spend unprofitably away or to refresh myself with recreations."[23] Although he was clearly a public benefactor, the businessman had put the increase of his own wealth above the common good. Of course, he would not be the last to do so.

A SOFTENING SENSE OF SIN

After the first generation, the wilderness had been largely cleared, the frontier rolled back, and the towns were secure. In time, comfort and luxury gradually intruded on Puritan life. The sons born in America had not experienced the labors of their immigrant fathers. As historian Herbert W. Schneider notes, "their fathers' strenuous standards began to irritate them, and the philosophy of God's wonder-working providence began to take on a hollow sound."[24]

The founding generation in turn complained of the worldliness of their offspring. Although the original practical value of the early moral standards was less conspicuous in the lives of later Puritans, the elders enacted prohibitions and restraining laws. Time-wasting now became inherently sinful and diversions subject to divine wrath as well as censure by church and state.

Of course, the consciences of later generations of Puritans were not so keen as their fathers', and for good reason. Although the ministers condemned worldliness, even they took pride in the colony's prosperity. A typical sermon exulted:

O generation see! Look upon your towns and fields, look upon your habitations and shops and ships, and behold your numerous prosperity, and great increase in the blessings of the land and sea; Have I been a wilderness unto you? We must needs answer, No, Lord, Thou hast been a gracious God, and exceeding good unto thy servants, even in these earthly blessings; we live in a more plentiful and comfortable manner than ever we did expect.[25]

Already, in the Cambridge Platform of 1648, it had been agreed that children be accepted as church members, but they were still expected to make a public profession of personal regeneration as adults before being admitted to Holy Communion. Many second-generation Puritans opted not to make that profession, yet they considered themselves church members and asked that their own children be baptized. Soon the majority of churchgoers in the colony were technically unregenerate persons known as baptized adult noncommunicants.

In 1698, a group of prominent, educated, and wealthy Bostonians established an independent church in Brattle Square. As their minister, they engaged Benjamin Coleman, who had been ordained by the Presbytery in London and was therefore not subject to colonial church authorities. Coleman dispensed altogether with the need for public profession and extended communion to all. He redefined local congregations as "societies of Christians by mutual agreement." To be Christian, one merely "professed faith in and obedience to Christ" and avoided "scandalous sin." "In other words," Schneider notes, "these respectable Yankees wished thenceforth to be known as Christian, not as unregenerates."[26] As other "genteel" congregations were formed, sin slowly slipped from the colony's lexicon.

AN EMBARRASSMENT OF WITCHES

Hawthorne's Hester Prynne was only a character in fiction, but the witches of Salem were real people, and their trials and executions forever taint our esteem for the Puritan experiment. Serious historians ask that we not condemn a whole people for what the scholars consider an aberration. Morison called the Salem with-hunt "a small incident in the history of a great superstition,"[27] and Perry Miller suggested that, with minor qualifications, "the intellectual history of New England can be written as though no such thing ever happened."[28]

But it happened, and it said something about the effects of moral repression on the Puritans. The first recorded witchcraft trial took place at Windsor, Connecticut in 1647. During the balance of the century there were nearly 100 cases. Thirty-eight people were executed as witches; a few more, though convicted, managed to escape the death penalty. The infamous trials at Salem in 1692 were urged by Cotton Mather, who subsequently defended the proceedings in his book, *The Wonders of the Invisible World.*

The witches were typically married or widowed women between the ages of forty-one and sixty, but there were a few men and younger women, usually the husbands or daughters of middle-aged female witches. Witchcraft was assumed to run in families. The vast majority of their accusers were adolescent girls. Some eighty-four persons came forward as "witnesses" during the Salem trials, three-fourths of them men, probably because it was rare for women to appear in court.

Historian John Demos notes that the persons accused of witchcraft were typically eccentric, "unusually irascible and contentious in their personal relations."[29] William Hubbard, who wrote his *General History of New England* even before the Salem trials, warned that "persons of hard favor and turbulent passions are apt to be condemned by the common people as witches, upon very slight grounds."[30] Adolescent girls in New England were subject to the control of older women and prone to resent their harsh or unpredictable behavior.

Contentiousness, of course, ran counter to the Puritan emphasis on community and cooperation. Most accusers were neighbors of the accused, and the very threat of being called a witch was used as a form of social constraint on difficult people. Demos notes that most witchcraft episodes followed an actual quarrel or attack. The accusers themselves displayed bizarre behavior, which we now would characterize as hysterical, but which they blamed on the satanical powers of the older women.

Anthropologists note that a belief in witchcraft is common among societies that impose severe restrictions on children's aggressive impulses.

Demos finds it significant that The Puritans found the specific complaints of the accusers so credible:

The accusers, then, can be viewed as those individuals who were somehow especially sensitive to the problems created by their environment; they were the ones who were pushed over the line, so to speak, into serious illness. But their behavior struck an answering chord in a much larger group of people. In this sense, nearly everyone in seventeenth-century New England was at some level an accuser.[31]

THE PERSISTENCE OF PURITANISM

By the time Massachusetts ceased being a colony and became a state, Puritan control of its society was only a memory. Yet Puritan values figured in the Constitution of the new nation. The vaunted "balance of powers" in our political life reflects the Puritans' suspicions about human nature. James Madison in his framing of the Constitution was sensitive to the Calvinist theology he acquired as a student at Princeton. Both he and Jefferson were students of the Enlightenment, but suspicious of self-interest in the new nation.

On the eve of the American Revolution, Abigail Adams echoed the Puritan belief in human depravity when she urged her husband, the nation's second president, to sponsor legislation that would protect women from the abuse of men. "That your sex are naturally tyrannical is a truth so thoroughly established as to admit of no dispute," she wrote him. "Remember, all Men would be tyrants if they could."[32]

Chapter 3

The Quakers:
The Power of Friendly Persuasion

My friends...going over to plant and make outward plantations in America, keep your own plantations in your hearts, with the spirit and power of God, that your own vines and lilies be not hurt.[1]

George Fox

Rejecting the strictures and hierarchies of the Old World, the Quakers set about to create a community in America that was radically democratic and egalitarian. They had all of Pennsylvania, plus significant portions of the other original colonies, in which to create their heaven on earth.

The Quakers were peacemakers. Persuaded that there is "that of God" in every human being, they were tolerant of all faiths and opinions and determined to improve the quality of life for everyone. They rehabilitated prisoners, educated the ignorant, and ensured that every child was taught a trade. To this day, despite their modest numbers, they remain masters in conflict resolution and community building around the world.

Quaker State lingers as the brand name of a popular motor oil. But in colonial America, there truly was a Quaker state—Pennsylvania—as dominated by the adherents of the prophet George Fox as Utah would later be by the followers of Joseph Smith and Brigham Young. Taking root in the colonies in 1657, less than a decade after its founding in England, the nonconformist faith grew to exert a significant influence in at least ten colonies and suited the American character.

Barred from influence in Puritan Massachusetts and Anglican Virginia, the Quakers nevertheless dominated religious and political life elsewhere in the New World. For thirty-six terms, Quaker governors led Rhode Island. By 1700 half the population of Newport was Quaker. Moreover, "Friends," as they called one another, were, until 1701 the only organized religious denomination in North Carolina. In addition to controlling Pennsylvania by royal charter, they governed West Jersey and East Jersey until they were combined into a single royal colony.

With the waning of Puritan orthodoxy, large Quaker populations settled in southern and western Massachusetts. By sheer force of numbers, they were influential in the social and political life of Maine, New Hampshire, New York City, Long Island, and towns around Boston. Moreover, by 1780, there were 3,000 Friends in Maryland and 5,000 in Virginia. In the middle of the eighteenth century, the Quaker population in America exceeded than that in Great Britain.

THE HOLY EXPERIMENT

In 1681, in settlement of a debt owed by King Charles II to his father, the English Quaker William Penn received a charter for the colony that came to bear his family name. Penn, persuaded that his charter came not from a king but from divine providence, determined to establish a model Christian community as a "Holy Experiment." He established a democratically elected Assembly, as well as freedom of conscience and the right to worship according to one's own convictions, discouraged bureaucracy, and abolished tithes.

Pennsylvania's prisons became workhouses for self-reform. All children to the age of twelve were taught a useful trade or skill. As far as possible consistent with the laws of the mother country, Penn also severely restricted slavery and the death penalty in the colony. The Holy Experiment clearly succeeded in this: it proved that religious tolerance was not inimical to political stability.

Quaker character stood in sharp contrast to that of the Puritans. Where the Pilgrims were exclusive, dogmatic, hierarchical, righteous, and quick to persecute dissent, Fox's followers were democratic, informal, mystical, tolerant, and nonviolent. Fearless missionaries, they openly sought persecution as validation of their faith. In Fox's own lifetime, Quakers took their faith to Ireland, France, Italy, Germany, Holland, Denmark, Surinam, Turkey, and the West Indies, as well as to America.

Friends believed that all persons of both sexes and all races and nationalities were equal in God's sight and deserved to be treated equally.

Quakers were neighborly with native Americans, purchasing rather than stealing land from them, and finding a kinship between tribal beliefs and their own.

Back in Great Britain Fox's followers were excluded from politics and the professions. As a consequence, they achieved prominence in business and science. By contrast, in the New World—especially in Pennsylvania—they were *required* to govern. As it turned out, certain articles of the Quaker faith, applied too literally, impeded their ability to rule those fellow citizens who did not share their religious convictions.

Quaker historian Rufus Jones identifies his coreligionists' supreme passion as "the cultivation of inward religion and an outward life consistent with the vision of their souls."[2] With the Puritans, Quakers shared a hatred of tyranny, plus a moral earnestness reminiscent of the Old Testament prophets, pitting the life of the spirit against that of the world.

THE QUAKER "PRINCIPLE"

With growing affluence, the Puritans softened their dogmatism and made compromises with plain living. The Quakers, by contrast, embraced simplicity and plain living with an almost fetish-like grasp. Unlike the Puritans, the Friends were religiously tolerant, but like them, they were anything but indifferent about their convictions, which they held tenaciously, ultimately to the detriment of their ability to rule a multiethnic and cultural Pennsylvania.

Whereas the Puritans had sought to build their ideal City upon a Hill by adherence to Old Testament strictures, the Quakers were persuaded that they could establish the kingdom of God on earth by personal obedience to inward Divine revelation. They felt that they had rediscovered a Principle (always spelled with a capital P) that could revolutionize life on earth. That Principle was the presence of a Divine Light in every person, no matter how sophisticated or uneducated, that directly revealed God's will to him or her, and called for acceptance.

Rufus Jones acknowledges that the colonial Quakers risked everything they had on the truth of this Principle of direct personal experience of the will of God. They were persuaded that by obedience to the prompting of the Holy Spirit, they could create the Peaceable Kingdom in their time and place, where the lamb would lie with the lion unmolested.

By thrift, fair dealing, and hard work, the Friends fast made early Pennsylvania the most prosperous and peaceful of the colonies. "From a wilderness," the Quaker Richard Townsend noted in 1727, "the Lord, by his good hand of Providence, hath made it a fruitful field."[3] But before long, as historian Daniel Boorstin observes,

the Quakers realized that their religious doctrines, if construed strictly, would put difficulties in the way of their running a government. It was one thing to live by Quaker principles, quite another to rule by them.[4]

Boorstin argues that the Quakers crippled their political and evangelical effectiveness "not by being false to their teachings, but by being too true to them."[5] In the tradition of the Gospel, the great Quaker prophets had opted for the spirit of the law over its letter, but succeeding generations of followers increasingly preferred the strict letter as proof of their faithfulness.

FROM EXPANSION TO CONTRACTION

Quakerism, on its surface, disdains dogma and rejects creeds as formulas that obscure God's direct and personal revelation to humankind. Nevertheless, some beliefs common to Friends compromised their ability to govern. For example, Fox himself took literally Jesus' prohibition of oath taking:

I say to you, don't use an oath at all. Don't swear by Heaven for it is God's throne, nor by the earth for it is his footstool, nor by Jerusalem for it is the city of the great King. No, and don't swear by your own head, for you cannot make a single hair white or black! Whatever you have to say let your "yes" be a plain "yes" and your "no" a plain "no"—anything more than this has a taint of evil.[6]

As it turned out, Great Britain came to accommodate individual Quakers by allowing them to substitute an "affirmation" for an oath. But in Pennsylvania, Quaker officials refused to administer oaths to non-Quakers in their jurisdictions, making it impossible for them to act as witnesses in trials of persons accused of crimes. The officials' position hardened to the point where they persuaded themselves that oaths were not only unnecessary to ensure honesty in courts of law but were evil in themselves.

Quaker pacifism also hardened into political principle, making it difficult to ensure the peace and protect the Pennsylvania populace from Native American, French, and domestic violence within their borders. While acknowledging that the fundamental duty of any government is to protect the people, Quaker members of the Pennsylvania Assembly (then a majority) could not bring themselves to compromise their peace testimony to actually ensure peace even by defensive use of arms.

After the first great wave of world evangelization, Friends in their private lives became increasingly content to survive as a "faithful remnant" rather than as prophets of the worldwide faith envisaged by George Fox. Plain dress, originally a Quaker protest against fickle fashion and luxury, in time became a uniform that set off Friends from their neighbors as a "peculiar people." So, too, was the Quaker insistence on quaint speech— addressing both the high and the lowly with the familiar "thee" and "thou" rather than the formal "you." Originally the custom meant only to underscore the equal dignity of all men and women before God, but it came to be a quaint fetish that distanced Quakers from their fellow Americans.

MARGINALIZATION

From being expansive, Quakerism shrank into itself. Originally attracted to quiet worship, Friends soon embraced silence as the *only* acceptable liturgy. Together with the tendency to confine their testimony within the walls of their meeting houses (rather than proclaiming it to the world), Friends focused on their orthodoxy. They became increasingly prone to expel members whose businesses had failed or who were too prominent in non-Quaker society. Moreover, they refused to sanction the marriages of Friends to non-Quakers.

Over time, these reactionary developments prompted a severe shrinkage in membership and the effective marginalization of the Quaker community in American society. Where Fox and his fellow prophets had attracted 60,000 members in their first decade of preaching the faith, today there are fewer than 17,000 active Friends in all of Great Britain. At present in the United States, there are perhaps 200,000 Quakers. It has taken 350 years to merely double the numbers that the founders converted in the first ten years.

When the Puritans in Great Britain overthrew the monarchy and proclaimed a commonwealth under Oliver Cromwell, William Penn fell out of favor in the mother country and went into hiding. After the restoration under Charles II, Pennsylvania came under royal governance for two years (1692–94), primarily because the colonial Quakers refused to cooperate in their colony's defense.

Although Penn voluntarily diminished his executive power as governor in favor of the Quaker-dominated Assembly, his coreligionists proved to be ungrateful. Penn's eldest son effectively renounced his father's religious faith, and the governor's steward was discovered to have defrauded the great man of the bulk of his wealth.

Discouraged, Penn sought to sell the Holy Experiment. Ten years later, on the verge of a sale, Penn suffered a crippling stroke and lingered as an invalid for the six remaining years of his life. During that time, Pennsylvania was held in trusteeship because of its founder's debts. On his death, it passed to his second wife, Hannah.

For all their tolerance, prosperity, and good intentions, the Pennsylvania Quakers possessed neither the taste nor the flair for governing. Increasingly, they took George Fox's counsel literally, embracing the "plantations in their hearts" in preference to the outward plantations they had founded and could have governed if they had made modest compromises for the benefit of non-Quakers in the colony.

Daniel Boorstin, the distinguished former Librarian of Congress, believes the Quaker faith and spirit prefigured the common faith of Americans at the founding of the nation and that it could have become the spiritual faith of the United States.[7] Unhappily, the faith turned in on itself as quickly and as soundly as it had originally turned outward to convert the world.

The fervor was still there, but now it was for perfection rather than persuasion.

THE PENCHANT FOR MARTYRDOM

In its first generations, Friends literally sought martyrdom. English Quakerism began as a protest movement, and it was a religious protest that they first exported to the colonies. In this they were unlike other immigrants, including the Puritans, who came to the New World to pursue their own orthodoxies unmolested. William Dewbury, who arranged for the passage of Quakers to America, professed that he "as joyfully entered prisons as palaces, and in the prison-house I sang praises to my God and esteemed the bolts and locks upon me as jewels."[8]

Boorstin marvels at the earliest Friends in America: "Never was a reward sought more eagerly than the Quakers sought out their crown of thorns."[9] In their courage and persistence, he compares them to Cortes in his quest for the treasure of the Aztecs and to Ponce de Leon in his search for the Fountain of Youth.

Unhappy to remain where their faith was tolerated (as in Rhode Island), Quaker missionaries deliberately entered Massachusetts to preach in the Puritans' own churches. Christopher Holder, known as the valiant apostle of New England Quakerism, is exemplary. In September 1657, a year after his arrival in America from England, he interrupted a church service in Salem to plead the Quaker faith. He had already been expelled for an earlier missionary visit.

This time he was seized by the hair, had a glove and kerchief stuffed into his mouth, and, with a Quaker companion, was confronted by the governor in Boston, who gave them thirty stripes each, confined them to a bare cell for three days and nights without bedding, food, and water, then imprisoned them for nine weeks in winter without heat. During that time, they were whipped twice a week, starting with fifteen stripes, adding three more during each subsequent punishment.

On his release, Holder was put on a ship to Barbados, where he continued to preach, but he returned to Massachusetts the next year. Arrested in Dedham, he was taken to Boston, where the Puritan authorities cut off one of his ears. Enraged at the persistence of the Quaker interlopers, in 1658, the Puritans narrowly enacted the death penalty as punishment for their preaching. Just a year later, they were confronted with the greatest of the Quaker martyrs, Mary Dyer.

In all likelihood, Mary was the daughter of a woman who, on the death of Elizabeth I, had a claim to the English throne. When James VI of Scotland took the throne of England as James I, Mary was entrusted to the care of a servant for her protection. As a young woman she married and settled in Puritan New England, where her husband became prominent in the life of the colony. She, however, was outspoken and became an irritant to the Pilgrim fathers. Accordingly, the Dyers settled with Roger Williams in Rhode Island and prospered.

On an extended trip to England, Mary met George Fox, embraced the Quaker faith, and determined to carry it back to Massachusetts. After an initial attempt to preach to the Puritans, she was banished from the colony under threat of execution. Returning, she was tried together with two male Quaker companions. Governor Endicott devoted a sermon to damning them, then pronounced the death sentence. "Yea, joyfully I shall go" to the gallows, Mary proclaimed. "It is an Hour of the greatest Joy I can enjoy in this World."[10]

After her companions were hanged, she was bound hand and foot, and her face covered by a handkerchief, then to her dismay was reprieved. The charade had been planned earlier in Massachusetts General Court to frighten her and ensure the success of her banishment. Mary's response was to refuse the reprieve unless the law that allowed the death penalty for Quakers was repealed. Less than a year later, on May 21, 1660, she returned to Boston, provoking the Puritans, mounted the gallows, and once again was offered a reprieve if she would only leave the colony forever. "Nay," she replied, "I cannot....In obedience to the will of the Lord God I came and in his will I abide faithful to death."[11]

This time she was hanged and became the first American martyr to religious freedom.

FRIENDLY PERSUASION

If the first generation of Quakers appeared to go out of their way to invite persecution for their convictions, in truth their faith could not have been more benign and pacific. They and their progeny were of a friendly persuasion—plain-speaking and plain-living, truthful, fair, generous, democratic, and peace-loving.

Like the Puritans, the Quakers held private property but styled their lives in close communion with other Friends, with the Meeting as the focal point of community life. Like the Puritans, they did not disdain business, and many Quakers in Britain and the colonies prospered. But there the similarities ended. Even well-to-do Friends lived simply, and they were known as fair employers and generous supporters of the larger community, building hospitals and schools and asylums.

Compared to the Church of England's liturgy, Puritan worship was stark, focussed on Scripture and sermon. But Quaker worship was stripped utterly bare. A meeting house was nothing more than an unadorned open room with benches. Moreover, Quakers dispensed with clergy, sacraments, sermons, and singing—not considering them to be pernicious, but unnecessary and potentially distracting. Worship consisted of the silent expectation of personal revelation within the group. Some Friends might speak up if they felt prompted by the Spirit, but not to preach—just to inspire others, typically couching their thoughts in the words of Scripture.

Without clergy or staff, Friends literally accepted the Protestant notion of the "priesthood of all believers." They ministered to one another, governed themselves, and maintained the meeting house with their own labor. In everything, Quaker women were equal to the men. Without reference to a creed, Quaker orthodoxy rested on precedent and the common inclination to discover God in everyone, to be simple, fair-dealing, truthful, and peacemaking. After the first great wave of evangelization, Quakers practiced their friendly persuasion through personal example, welcoming new Friends to their family, but they ceased proselytizing, preferring to let God do the leading. Their reticence, of course, was not a formula for growth.

THE PROBLEM WITH PACIFISM

"Let us do our duty, and leave the rest to God,"[12] William Penn counseled his fellow Pennsylvanians in 1701. But it became increasingly problematic for the Quakers to govern dutifully and still pursue the purity of their faith. A century later, Thomas Jefferson referred to American Quakers as

a religious sect...acting with one mind, and that directed by the mother society in England. Dispersed, as the Jews, they still form, as those do, one nation, foreign to the land they live in. They are Protestant Jesuits, implicitly devoted to the will of their superior, and forgetting all duties to their country in the execution of the policy of their order.[13]

It was a harsh judgment on a people who were as democratically disposed, fair-minded, and as religiously tolerant as Jefferson himself.

It is true that the London Yearly Meeting constantly intervened to shape Quaker policy in the colonies to serve the interests of the international community of Friends, sending emissaries to press the Americans to accept rigid orthodoxy. There was to be no compromise on taking or administering oaths, or on pacifism and capital punishment.

Daniel Boorstin observes that "whenever tested, the Quakers chose the solution which kept themselves pure, even though others might have to pay the price."[14] As to pacifism, the Pennsylvania Friends attempted for a century to evade the issue by ensuring that their Deputy-Governor be a congenial non-Quaker. In effect, it was he who provided for the colony's common defense, leaving the pacifist consciences of the Quaker-dominated Assembly untainted.

When, in April 1689, England declared war against the French and instructed the Quakers to defend their colony and establish a militia, a member of Penn's Council scoffed, saying there was no danger to Pennsylvanians except from "the bears and wolves." A dozen years later England was fighting both France and Spain. The war was duly proclaimed in Pennsylvania, but the Quaker Assembly politely refused to raise funds for defense, noting politely:

Were it not that the raising money to hire men to fight or kill one another is matter of Conscience to us and against our Religious Principles, we should not be wanting, according to our small abilities, to Contribute to those designs.[15]

When a new war began in 1739, Spanish privateers sailed on the Delaware threatening the colony. Rather than raising a militia in Pennsylvania's defense or to provision an English garrison, the Quakers in the Assembly preferred to paralyze the government, preventing any legislation. For a time in 1741, they even withheld the governor's salary.

When, in 1745, the governor finally wrested an appropriation to provision English troops, he was careful to mention only food, not arms.

THE WITHDRAWAL FROM POWER

From the outset, the Quakers had treated the Indians fairly and generously, seeking to cultivate their friendship. But the Indians were not altogether pacific. Rather, they warred tribe against tribe and harassed isolated settlers. Some took sides against the English colonists during the French and Indian War. Despite massacres in Western Pennsylvania, the Quaker-dominated Assembly made a large cash gift to the Indians in 1748, meanwhile refusing to provide for the defense of Philadelphia. When Pennsylvania forged an alliance in 1742 with the Iroquois, the Delawares considered it a provocation.

By 1745, a strong compromise party emerged in the Assembly, led by Benjamin Franklin. It was neither pro- nor anti-Quaker, but insisted on the duty of the colonial government to protect the citizenry. If the Quaker legislators could not do so on principle, Franklin's party argued, then they should allow others to rule and defend Pennsylvania. Franklin himself managed to raise private funds to form and equip a militia of 10,000 men. It proved inadequate. A decade later Franklin lamented that "our frontier people (are) continually butchered," and concluded, "I do not believe we shall ever have a firm peace with the Indians, till we have well drubbed them."[16]

ABDICATION

Franklin's popular party proposed making all male colonists subject to military duty, commutable by a fine. Militia officers would be democratically elected. According to the proposal, Quakers would not have to bear arms themselves but would have to help pay for the colony's defense. By 1756, although Friends comprised fewer than one-fourth of all Pennsylvanians, Quakers still held more than three-fourths of the seats in the colonial Assembly and ignored Franklin's appeal.

Meanwhile, the English government, concerned for the protection of the colonists, proposed permanently disqualifying Quakers from holding public office in Pennsylvania. Dr. John Fothergill, a respected elder of London Yearly Meeting, spelled out the governor's case against the Quaker legislators:

...you are unfit for government. You accept our publick trust, which at the same time you acknowledge you cannot discharge. You owe the people protection, & yet withhold them from protecting themselves. Will not all the blood that is spilt lye at your doors? and can we...sit still and see the province in danger of being given up to a merciless enemy without endeavoring its rescue?[17]

London Quakers negotiated with the English government to permit members of the colonial Assembly to resign voluntarily, then sent John Hunt and Christopher Wilson to persuade their coreligionists in Pennsylvania to do so. In late spring of 1756, the governor and his council declared war on the Shawnee and Delaware Indians, which forced the issue. Quaker members abdicated rather than support their colony's armed defense, and the colony passed permanently into governance by non-Quakers.

In this respect, the Holy Experiment came to an end, although many Quaker politicians believed they could regain office once hostilities ended. But when the American Revolution commenced some twenty years later, Quakers were once again compromised. Although they refused to pay taxes and fines to the nascent American government, many Friends continued to pay duties to England and were thus branded Tories and traitors to the cause of freedom.

Increasingly withdrawn from public life, they tended the "plantations in their hearts," setting even stricter standards for themselves, becoming a "peculiar people." In their quest for inner perfection, they sought to remove and forbid tombstones as vanities, forbade intermarriage, decried the use of alcohol, and increased religious instruction in Quaker schools. No longer in government themselves, they discouraged Friends from taking disputes to courts of law, preferring arbitration within the Meeting itself. However, they did not withdraw altogether from public life. Rather, their missionary spirit was reinvested in campaigns against slavery and the slave-trade, in the reform of prisons and asylums, in the construction of hospitals, and in increasing justice.

A MISSED OPPORTUNITY

Quakers suffered from an early ambivalence about education. Eventually they rectified it, but too late to leave a significant mark on American culture. Harvard, Yale, and William and Mary were founded as seminaries to support the established churches of their respective colonies. But when the College of Philadelphia (now the University of Pennsylvania) was founded, it was not by Quakers but by a coalition of Anglicans and Presbyterians.

Friends, of course, had no need of seminaries, because they had no clergy. Moreover, as Rufus Jones explains, "the Quaker naturally and logically looked upon the true minister as a passive and oracular 'instrument' of the Holy Spirit...not a teacher or an interpreter (but) a revealer through whom Divine Truth was 'opened.'" George Fox had favored the creation of educational institutions to teach everything "civil and useful in the creation," but his followers were slow to comply, with the consequence that (in Jones' words) "no adequate education for Quaker youth was available (and) they soon found themselves largely cut off from the great currents of culture."[18]

The problem was the early Friends' failure to regard the revelation of knowledge, either divine or human, as more than passive. As Jones laments:

Their failure to appreciate the importance of the fullest expansion of human personality by education is the primary cause of their larger failure to win the commanding place in American civilization of which their early history gave promise. Their central Principle, properly understood, called for a fearless education, for there is no safety in individualism, in personal responsibility, or in democracy, whether in civil or religious matters, unless every individual is given a chance to correct his narrow individualism in the light of larger groups...[19]

Penn himself demonstrated the early Quaker ambivalence toward learning. Although he possessed a substantial personal library, he famously warned his children to "have but few books," arguing that "more true knowledge comes by Meditation and just Reflection than by Reading; for much Reading is an Oppression of the Mind, and extinguishes the natural Candle; which is the Reason of so many senseless Scholars in the World."[20]

Nevertheless, Philadelphia became arguably the most civilized and cultured city in the new nation. At the beginning of the Revolution, it boasted seventy-seven bookshops—second only to London in the English book trade. The Friends' religious tolerance welcomed peoples of many faiths, enriching the community. By 1759, Philadelphia had three Quaker meetings and two Presbyterian churches, as well as a society of Freemasons, and Lutheran, Dutch Calvinist, Swedish, and Roman Catholic churches, plus Anabaptist and Moravian meeting houses.

THE LIVING LEGACY

If the Holy Experiment did not precisely succeed in establishing Penn's vision of heaven on earth in the New World, it nevertheless demonstrated the civilizing tendencies that would combine to form the American character. The Declaration of Independence was conceived and published in Philadelphia, and the City of Brotherly Love became the first capital of a new nation conceived in liberty and dedicated to the proposition that all men are created equal with inalienable rights—surely articles of Quaker faith. The original Quaker-drafted constitution of Rhode Island became the model for the Bill of Rights.

The contemporary Quaker historian John Punshon notes that

Pennsylvania became a beacon of hope for all who shared the Quakers' belief in equality and human dignity; the relations of the Commonwealth with the Indians redeemed in some small measure the many atrocities otherwise visited on the Native Americans; the penal code was unparalleled in its humanity at the time. Out of the vision of one man and his religious Society sprang an application of those principles that would soon lead to the creation of American democracy, and an assurance for lovers of freedom everywhere that their hope was not in vain.[21]

To this day, Quakers enjoy a worldwide influence out of all proportion to their modest numbers, probably because they have no ideology to press and no axes to grind. They enter international crises but do not take sides. During the 1930s, Quakers met with Adolf Hitler's representatives in an effort to forestall the holocaust. Undeterred, their efforts to relieve the suffering of the German people after World War II won the American Friends Service Committee the Nobel Peace Prize.

When conflicts arise and natural tragedies occur around the world, Quakers are not always the first on the scene to relieve human suffering, but they are typically the last to leave. It is the Friends' experience that food, medicine, and shelter are not enough. People need to be reconciled with one another, and Quakers are masters of friendly persuasion. Wherever tragedy strikes in the world, Friends not only work with other international relief agencies but also seek to meet needs the others neglect. In Kosovo, they stayed behind to rebuild public libraries and to reconcile the Serbs and ethnic Albanians. In the Afghan winter of 2002, they collected and shipped tens of thousands of blankets for the homeless refugees.

A PENCHANT FOR SERVICE

Relieved of the burden of governance, Friends came to exert more influence than ever over the quality of life in America and beyond. They produced saints—dedicated, heroic, confident, humble, and loving—as simple in their affections as in their dress and demeanor. Unburdened of clergy and church hierarchy, they sensed themselves to be citizens of the Church Invisible, equal in God's sight, personally responsible to minister to all in need. Freed from the burden of a comprehensive creed, they concentrated on the core requirements of religious faith—loving God and serving humankind.

The type was exemplified by John Woolman, who by friendly persuasion, caused Quakers to free their slaves and wakened the conscience of the young nation to the dignity God imparted to every man, woman, and child, regardless of belief, race, education, or station in life.

"The real glory of this movement," writes the Quaker Rufus Jones,

was the "levelling up" of an entire people...Farmers, with hands made rough by the plough-handle, in hundreds of rural localities not only preached messages of power on meeting days, but also, what is more to the point, lived daily lives of radiant goodness in simple neighborhood service. Women who had slight chances for culture, and who had to do the hard work of pioneer housewifery, by some subtle spiritual alchemy, were transformed into a virile sainthood, which made itself felt both in the Sunday gathering and in the unordained care of souls throughout the community. It was a real experiment in the "priesthood of believers"...[22]

From the outset, the effectiveness of Quakers was multiplied by its women, who served as ministers and missionaries. After the early period of evangelization ended, Friends of both sexes became powerful advocates for child welfare, prison reform, public health and education, civil rights, peace, reconciliation, reconstruction, universal suffrage, and justice to minorities. Susan B. Anthony credited her Quaker upbringing as motivating her successful quest for woman suffrage.

Today the Friends Committee on National Legislation is one of the most effective lobbying organizations in the Nation's Capital, precisely because it has no selfish interest or agenda. Similarly, the American Friends Service Committee makes no demand on the millions of desperate people around the world which it assists. It simply exists to serve.

In these important respects, Penn's Holy Experiment was clearly a success.

Chapter 4

The Amish: Return to Paradise

I completely abandoned myself to the Lord.[1]

Anabaptist martyr, 1527

Unlike the cloister, the Puritans, and the Quakers—which are utopian movements—the Amish are a utopian *fellowship* composed of more than 650 communities in America alone.

Their long legacy of persecution has long since persuaded them to build their heaven on earth apart from the rest of society. They do not aspire to export their values, but only to exemplify them in their own sequestered communities.

Despite their drastic rejection of contemporary technology and convenience, the Amish offer lessons for the restoration of community in the society beyond their enclaves—in family and fellowship, mutual aid, sanctity of labor, and reverence for life.

Lancaster County, Pennsylvania, bears no resemblance to Disney's Magic Kingdom. It is merely the most prosperous agricultural county in America. Yet each year, it attracts over five million tourists, few of whom express any interest in farming. Instead they come to catch the sight of a peculiar people who have contrived a simple, devout life that few moderns would even consider to be emulating.

They are the Old Order Amish. While there are more than 14,000 of them in Lancaster County alone, they are much more than a local peculiarity. Dispersed across North America, there are 660 Amish congregations in twenty states plus the Canadian province of Ontario. Seven in ten are concentrated in the three adjacent states of Indiana, Ohio, and Pennsylvania.

Although they seek no converts, the Amish are growing in numbers. Because their faith is founded on the sanctity of the family, Amish wives traditionally welcome as many children as God might provide. Since the sect considers contraception to be an affront to the Creator's gift of life, the average Amish couple bears 6.6 sons and daughters—nearly three times the American average. One in seven Amish families has ten or more children.

Although the Amish are the magnets who draw tourists to Lancaster County, they are a private and elusive people. It is just possible that a visitor will not catch sight of one at all unless he passes a horse and buggy on a county road and glimpses a long-bearded driver and his plain-dressed wife on their way to market.

Each year there are 350 visitors for every Amish person. The tourists spend over $400 million each year to witness the faith and absorb the culture of these plain people who have created their own heaven on earth.

Ironically, the Amish themselves profit hardly at all from tourism. The Pennsylvania Dutch Visitors' Bureau, run by outsiders, is strictly commercial, featuring attractions that promise much more than the Amish themselves care to deliver. No genuine Amish farm or home is open to tourists. At most, Amish wives may sell farm products and quilts by the roadside. But local entrepreneurs have created replicas of Amish homesteads and sell food, lodging, tours, crafts, and trinkets that they promote as authentic. Like animals in a zoo, the Amish are the attraction but do not share the price of admission.

The intrusions on Amish life probably reached their peak in the spring of 1984, when Paramount Pictures came to Lancaster County to film *Witness,* a thriller starring Harrison Ford, playing a Philadelphia detective who finds refuge with an Amish family and romances a young widow, played by Kelly McGillis. The script called for a violent shoot-out finale on an Amish farm.

The pacifist Amish, who considered Hollywood to be the purveyor of worldliness, were stunned by the intrusion and the glorification of violence. Although no Amish were employed in the cast, Kelly McGillis disguised herself to spend several days in an Amish home to research her role. Once identified, she was evicted. "We can't stop them," one Amishman said, "but we don't have to help them. We don't want it. It doesn't belong here."[2] Perversely, the completed film purported to portray violence and hateful speech within the peace-loving Amish community itself.

A LEGACY OF PERSECUTION

The elusiveness of the Amish is probably part of their charm, but their separation from the world is rooted in their faith and in centuries of persecution. Their forebears were Swiss Anabaptists who were unhappy with the pace of the Protestant Reformation. Upstart students of Pastor Ulrich Zwingli rebuked him and the Zurich City Council for continuing to baptize infants and celebrate the Mass. They maintained instead that only adults can make the personal commitment of obedience to Jesus that is fundamental to baptism.

The rebels were nicknamed Anabaptists or "rebaptizers," because they had already been christened in the Roman Catholic Church. Their belief in the absolute authority of Scripture marked them for persecution by both civil and religious authorities. Over the course of two centuries in Switzerland, Germany, and the Netherlands, thousands of Anabaptists became victims of torture, branding, burning, drowning, imprisonment, and dismembering for heresy and sedition. To this day, along with the family bible, many Amish homes display a copy of *The Martyrs Mirror,* a vast chronicle of the persecutions suffered by their ancestors in faith.

Although executions subsided in Switzerland by 1614, persecution continued for another century. Many Anabaptists became known as Mennonites, taking their name from Menno Simons, a converted Catholic priest. Sociologist Donald B. Kraybill notes that as early as 1527, the Anabaptists embraced the New Testament as their guide for everyday living. They stressed:

- literal obedience to the teachings of Christ,
- the church as a covenant community,
- adult baptism,
- physical and social separation from the evil world,
- expulsion of errant members from the community,
- rejection of physical and verbal violence, and
- refusal to swear oaths.[3]

Persecution drove the Anabaptists to remote areas of northern Europe, where they took up farming as a way to become economically and socially insulated from a hostile, sinful world.

The Amish emerged in the 1690s, when the Alsatian Anabaptist Jacob Ammann proposed that communion services be held twice rather than once a year, and that they include foot-washing as a corporate sign of humility. Ammann considered fashionable dress and the trimming of beards to be expressions of vanity, and even rejected buttons as ostentatious. To this day, the Amish fasten their clothing with hook-and-eye instead.

More controversial was Ammann's teaching that any excommunicated Anabaptist be shunned socially as well. Over this issue, the Amish broke from the Mennonites. Once baptized, an Amish man or woman is expected to remain faithful to his community for life. Once separated, even family members are forbidden to communicate with them.

BUILDING HEAVEN ON EARTH IN AMERICA

Mennonites were already in the New World in 1683, settled in Pennsylvania. The *Charming Nancy,* carrying the first large group of Amish, arrived in Philadelphia in 1737. The newcomers created two small communities near Lancaster. Both settlements were dismantled after raids by Indians, and the Amish dispersed to locate less vulnerable land. The county nevertheless remained a magnet for Amish immigration, and by 1880 was home to six congregational groups. Although a secure Mennonite presence in Lancaster continues to this day, the Amish purchased the best farmland in the county during the twentieth century and thrived. The county's 5,000 farms produce milk, eggs, poultry, meat, corn, hay, and tobacco, leading the state in agriculture.

Unlike communitarian utopias, the Amish base their paradise on family ownership of productive private property. While living in great simplicity, many Amish have become millionaires in terms of the market value of their properties. As a community pledged to mutual aid, no member goes in want. But the Amish avoid dependency on the outside world. When necessary, they borrow from commercial banks, but they turn aside government assistance, rejecting farm supports, social security, and Medicare.

All the social security they need they find in their faith, their families, and their Amish neighbors. Although they pay local property taxes to support the county's public schools, they do not use them. Instead, they send their offspring to one-room Amish schoolhouses that educate all Amish children through the eighth grade. After lengthy battles with state and federal authorities, the sect was exempted from sending their children to high schools. Their argument was that a child does not need secondary education to be a farmer. Moreover, they pleaded, consolidated high schools would expose Amish teenagers to skepticism and worldly values.

In their homes and in their conversations with one another, the Amish speak a German dialect, but classes in Amish schools are taught in English, and the children swiftly become fluent in the language of the outside community—a necessity for conducting business. The Amish avail themselves of lawyers, doctors, dentists, veterinarians, and other professionals in the secular community but have no aspiration for their children to be anything other than farmers and craftsmen. Rather than purchasing commercial insurance (which they consider gambling), they rely on one another's assistance when adversity strikes.

Amish teachers are typically bright unmarried women with no more than an eighth-grade education themselves. Married Amish women work at home. Single women in the community find employment, as needed, in the county's motels and restaurants, shops, and markets. Men labor in their fields and shops, and the entire focus of life is on the home.

Apart from their plain dress, the most striking distinction between the Amish and their neighbors is what they do without—electricity, automobiles, telephones, television, and commercial entertainment. The horse still pulls the plow in the Amish fields, where the tractor is taboo.

Contemporary Amish homes resemble those in the larger community and feature indoor plumbing. But they are lit by lanterns and lack central heating. An Amish kitchen includes refrigerator and range, but both run on bottled gas. There is no dishwasher. Laundry is washed by machines running on generators.

Of the Amish, Kraybill says, "Only by being a separate people have they been able to remain together, and only by shunning modernity have they been able to survive."

THE AMISH WAY OF LIFE

Considering the absence of modern conveniences and entertainment, and the emphasis on physical labor, one might predict that Amish children would part with tradition or at least compromise with the old ways. In fact, while they are aware of the allurements of the outside world, four out of five Amish boys and girls freely choose to remain members of the community for their entire adult lives.

The tenacity of commitment is explained by a religious faith founded on submission, self-surrender, resignation to God's will, and a yielding of oneself to God and to others. Amish life is marked by self-denial, contentment, and an untroubled spirit, and aided by habits of humility, thrift, simplicity, and love. Like all attempts to build heaven on earth, the Amish exchange individualism and competition for society and cooperation. For the Amish, personal fulfillment is found in devotion to God and the community.

The sect's members organize their lives to underscore faithfulness to God and to one another. Rather than attempting to change history, they trust God and are content with providence rather than progress. Modesty in dress, conversation, and action makes for peace. Smallness encourages neighborliness.

Their aim is the true imitation of Christ, who lived wholly for others and, lacking self-interest, suffered on their behalf. The Amish take the Sermon on the Mount as their moral compass, prizing simplicity, mercy, meekness, humility, peacemaking, and purity of heart. Reflecting their long legacy of persecution, they follow Christ's example, praying for their tormentors and loving their enemies. They take seriously Jesus' affirmation that only those who lose their lives will save them.

The history of secular as well as religious organizations suggests that those which require much from their members are most successful in retaining their loyalty, whereas undemanding groups are valued less highly. The Amish way of life is highly demanding, but its demonstrable success is founded on mutual assistance and separation from the temptations and conflicts of the world.

Renouncing the use of force in everyday dealings, the Amish reject military service and political office and do without courts, lawsuits, jury duty, and commercial competition. They reject personal ambition as contrary to Christ's example and submit to God-ordained leaders among their company.

Although they disdain worldliness, the Amish do not believe the material world or pleasure to be evil. Rather, in their estimation, self-love accounts for life's miseries. What the sect's members treasure is wholesomeness—good food, sexual love within marriage, affection within the family, friendship within the community, the beauty of nature, and the joy of physical labor and recreation.

FEW AND SMALL MIRRORS

The typical Amish home has few mirrors, and they are small. Kraybill observes:

Whereas Moderns are preoccupied with "finding themselves," the Amish are engaged in "losing themselves."[4]

Women foreswear cosmetics and wear their hair in a simple bun. Men's beards are untrimmed, but they shave their upper lip because they recall the vanity of military officers who cultivated moustaches in centuries past. Recall the Matthew Brady photo of the mature Abraham Lincoln, and you have a fair likeness of an Amish male.

With many children in the typical Amish family, each learns to wait for his or her turn. Sociologists have remarked that Amish boys and girls seldom begin a sentence with "I" or use the words "me," "myself," "my," or "mine." A standardized personality test given by researcher John Hostetler to Amish children revealed the typical child to be

quiet, friendly, responsible, and conscientious. Works devotedly to meet his obligations and serve his friends and school...patient with detail and routine. Loyal, considerate, concerned with how other people feel even when they are in the wrong.[5]

The Amish do not hesitate to spank their young children to underscore a lesson in acceptable behavior. Kraybill quotes an Amish leader:

By the time that child reaches the age of three the mold has started to form and it is the parents' duty to form it in the way that the child should go. When the child is old enough to stiffen its back and throw back its head in temper it is old enough to gently start breaking that temper.[6]

While suburban children are being ferried by parents to soccer games and music lessons to establish their individuality, Amish children are busy working in their homes and fields without a sense of deprivation. In Amish schools, JOY is a motto, meaning Jesus is first. You are last. Others are in between. Amish priorities are exemplified in these verses memorized in school:

I must be a Christian child,
Gentle, patient, meek, and mild;
Must be honest, simple, true
In my words and actions too.
I must cheerfully obey,
Giving up my will and way...[7]
Must remember, God can view
All I think, and all I do.
Glad that I can know I try,
Glad that children such as I,
In our feeble ways and small,
Can serve Him who loves us all.

SOWING WILD OATS

Still, Amish children—particularly the boys—are not exempt from the traditional turmoil of adolescence. Typical rebellion takes the form of flirting with worldliness—drinking, driving, and joining gangs of fellow Amish who indulge in parties and dances. As many as one-third of Amish teens own cars and even more have a driver's license. Some go to movies or take vacations, doffing plain Amish garb and donning fashions favored by teens outside the close community. These antics are an embarrassment to their parents and other elders, especially when the local police intervene in cases of drunk driving.

Nevertheless, Amish parents are philosophical about the rebellion, feeling that youth cannot reject worldliness unless they have tasted it and have found it wanting—which the vast majority do. The Amish belief in adult baptism means that, until they make the personal commitment, the youngsters are not members of the church and not strictly bound by its dictates. Kraybill suggests that the Amish elders' tolerance for adolescent antics is a way of giving the youngsters the impression that they have a real choice in determining how they will live the rest of their lives. The relatively few youths raised in Amish homes who indefinitely postpone baptism eventually leave the community, but they are not shunned because they have broken no vows.

For many children of Amish families, romance is a strong incentive for settling permanently into community and church. Living apart from the society outside, Amish boys and girls grow up together enjoying one another's company. An Amish couple cannot wed if one has not yet taken the baptismal vows. Kraybill quotes one young husband on his former flirtation with the world:

Most of the youth sowing wild oats are just out there to put on a show. . . . If they have well-established roots, most of them kind of have their mind set on a particular girl. There is something there that really draws them back. . . . The best I can explain is that it is strong family ties that really do pull. I had the world in front of me, but the other thing that I had, too, was the farm. I had the cows since I was 18 and was kind of tied down. . . . I will admit, I was rebellious enough. Like I say, the close family ties are the thing that really draws you back. . . . If you do a lot of this running around and going on, it kinda makes you feel foolish after awhile.[8]

JOINING AND WORSHIPPING

Amish youngsters typically apply for baptism between the ages of sixteen and twenty-one, after five months of weekly instructions on the duties of membership. The day before baptism the candidates are given their last chance to reconsider and are assured that it is better never to take a vow than to take it and break it.

Baptism is held following two sermons in the course of the regular Sunday morning service. Candidates kneel and consider "before the Most High and Almighty God and His church if you still think this is the right thing to do to obtain your salvation." They are asked three questions to which they answer yes:

1. Are you willing, by the help and grace of God, to *renounce* the world, the devil, your own flesh and blood, and be *obedient* only to God and his church?
2. Are you willing to walk with Christ and his church and to remain faithful through life and until death?
3. Can you confess that Jesus Christ is the Son of God?

Water is poured over the candidate's head and the bishop prays, "May the Lord God complete the good work which he has begun in you and strengthen and comfort you to a blessed end through Jesus Christ. Amen."[9]

Of course, the newly baptized are not new to worship, having joined their parents since early childhood. Amish services are held on alternate Sundays, rotating among the members' homes. The communities are kept small enough that each family hosts all the other members at least once during the course of a year. Amish homes are built with open floor plans to accommodate large numbers of people in admittedly cramped quarters. Partitions are opened to accommodate as many as 125 adults and a like number of children. Plain backless benches are brought by horse and wagon to the house of worship that week.

Services begin as early as 7:30 a.m. in the morning and end in a common meal at noon, with socializing thereafter. Men and women enter the house by separate doors and sit apart. The women prepare the common meal, eat at separate tables, and are responsible for cleanup. There are no liturgical props for worship, just sermons and singing without accompaniment. A hymn can endure as long as 20 minutes, a sermon last for over an hour. Sermons are spontaneous, delivered without reference to notes. Prayer is silent, with the community kneeling on the hard floor. Since the children receive their religious education during the week, they remain with the adults on Sunday. The Amish hymnal contains words only; everyone has long since memorized the tunes. Only ordained men stand or speak at the services.

The typical congregation includes an average thirty-three families, all living in close proximity to one another. They ordain their own ministers, who serve life terms without pay. A bishop, chosen from among the ministers, is responsible for two congregations. He presides over baptisms, weddings, and funerals, as well as Sunday worship. Because each congregation worships on alternate Sundays, the bishop is able to be present at every service. Many Amish worship with their sister congregation on open Sundays.

The typical congregation chooses two or three ministers from among their men, as well as a deacon, who reads from Scripture and is charged with mutual aid within the congregation. The deacon also investigates any reports of rule-breaking within members' families, delivering messages of excommunication and reinstatement to offenders. All these leaders, considered servants of the community, are not selected by ability or ambition but by lot.

COMMUNION AND CONFESSION

A communion service is held in fall and spring, typically for adult members only, and includes a lengthy sermon that chronicles God's activities from the creation to the defeat of Joshua's army, then turns to the teachings of Jesus. Members are encouraged to confess their hidden sins of pride and disobedience.

The service, which can last from 8 a.m. until 4 p.m., is preceded by a day of fasting, and culminates in the memorial sharing of bread and wine. As an expression of humility, members stoop to wash the feet of their brothers and sisters. In the weeks prior to communion, area bishops meet to assess the spiritual state of the entire community, ensuring that members are at peace and in agreement with Amish practices and prohibitions. Unless there is peace, communion is postponed.

Any backsliding members are visited privately by the deacon and urged to repent and comply. Offenses can range from using a tractor in the field to filing a lawsuit or attending a dance. If the wrong is acknowledged and the offender promises to stop, the matter is dropped.

Public confession is required, however, for a blatant public offense. Depending on the severity of the misdeed, the offender either sits or kneels before the congregation while being accused, then is allowed to tell his side of the story. The congregation's unanimous agreement is required to the bishop's proposal for penance. The most severe punishment is a six-week probationary separation from the community, during which the offender is shunned socially by all other members but is required to meet regularly with ministers for admonition. Unrepentant members can be excommunicated altogether, whereupon they are permanently shunned. Nevertheless, they are welcome to return to request reinstatement.

On occasion, members freely and openly confess their failings without prompting, seeking punishment. Kraybill recalls a young couple who volunteered that they indulged in sex before marriage. They asked to be expelled and shunned by the congregation for six weeks before being reinstated.

While firm about guaranteeing the purity of their community, the Amish are patient with offenders, working with them to try to win them back. Only in cases as public and blatant as adultery, divorce, or the purchase of an automobile is excommunication virtually assured. A bishop explains, "The ban is like the last dose of medicine that you can give to a sinner. It either works for life or death." For the Amish, who live so close to one another, shunning is the social equivalent of solitary confinement. A former Amishman acknowledged that "shunning works a little bit like an electric fence around a pasture with a pretty good fence charger on it."[10]

WHY THE AMISH PROHIBIT WHAT THEY DO

At first blush, Amish taboos appear arbitrary and pointless. In fact, they are practical ways of ensuring wholesome living within a tight faith-based community. The Amish are not Luddites bent on destroying machinery, but they believe that modern technologies of convenience erode the value of labor, appeal to vanity and luxury, and separate people. Far from being unthinking traditionalists, the Amish are flexible in accepting innovations so long as they do not endanger the quality of family and community life.

Amish farm life is based on the horse. Instead of an automobile and tractor, the typical Amish farm family has one or two road horses to pull buggies to town, and six to eight horses and mules to work in the fields. Relying on horse power limits travel and confines field work to daylight hours. It also keeps the Amish farm compact and insulates the farmer from the ambition to expand his acreage. The horse anchors the Amish to the land and to physical labor. It slows life down.

Although inconvenient, the horse is not unproductive. On smaller farms, the Amish are cost-competitive with mechanized farmers, who must purchase $40,000 tractors and $80,000 combines to cultivate their fields. The simple grey horse-drawn buggy, like Amish clothing, is a community standard that symbolizes Amish egalitarianism. There is no opportunity for choice or status as with automobiles. Automobiles are invitations to escape; the Amish choose to stay put.

Electricity is not altogether absent from Amish life, but the Amish resist its ready access because it opens people's lives to private convenience and entertainment rather than the pleasure of communal work and recreation. The Amish use batteries, as needed, notably for lights and signals on their buggies and for calculators. Moreover, they use gas-powered generators to drive hydraulic and air-pressure machines. Amish farmers sometimes drag modern plows and harvesters behind their horses.

By not connecting to power lines, the Amish underscore their independence from the outside community. Their disdain for central heating, even in contemporary houses, has another explanation. Central hearing, they reason, encourages members of a family to seek privacy in their own rooms. Using a butane space heater in a central room draws the family together.

Without electricity, the Amish are attuned to the normal passing of day into night, using efficient lanterns to illumine their homes, barns, and shops. Since electricity is needed for television, computers, dishwashers, video games, stereos, CD players, and an ever-expanding array of conveniences, the Amish avoid them all by rejecting the source of power.

The telephone is another matter. The Amish use them in emergencies and for making appointments in the outside world, but they do not keep them in their homes and barns. Instead, it is common in Amish country to install a community phone shanty at the end of a road, making phones available but not convenient.

When the telephone was first introduced into rural America, it alleviated the loneliness and isolation of farm life. The Amish argument against the telephone is that it has become a substitute for face-to-face socializing and spontaneous visiting among neighbors. As Kraybill notes,

The old adage "Its easier to say no on the phone than in person" captures the greater social distance and lower personal accountability underlying phone conversations.[11]

The prohibition against automobiles is not rigid. In necessity, Amish may hire someone to drive them, but they are not to own or drive themselves. Although Amish farmers receive supplies by truck, and Amish manufacturers ship by truck, there is no hypocrisy involved since they are not along for the ride. Doing without automobiles keeps the Amish at home.

THE AMISH IN TRANSITION

But it does not necessarily keep them on the farm. As Amish agriculture flourishes, the price of land has soared, doubling between 1973 and 1978.

By 1970, the Amish of Lancaster County faced a dilemma. Their birth rate had doubled their population in just twenty years. Traditionally, a farmer with three sons would purchase a farm for each of them, but now available land was shrinking and much was swept up by local developers and businesses associated with tourism. At the end of the 1960s, when eighty young Amish couples were married, only ten farms were available. How would they earn a living?

Parents could build homes for their children on their own property, but with only an eighth-grade education, what jobs were available to them, and would they have to leave farm and family to take them? An Amish bishop warned, "Leave this one generation grow up off the farm, and their sons won't want to farm." Fearful that working in factories would destroy Amish culture, he proclaimed, "The lunch pail is the greatest threat to our way of life."[12]

Outward migration was one solution, but ultimately unsatisfying, because it separates parents from their adult children. Still, by the early 1980s, 15 percent of the Amish had moved to farms in more affordable counties. Another solution was to subdivide existing farms and concentrate on specialized cash crops. But it was clear that the only acceptable long-term option was to move into commerce, preferably Amish-owned, farm-related industries that would employ men who had no farms of their own.

Today fully one-third of married Amishmen in Lancaster County are not farmers, but many of them work in shops on or near farms. Craftsmanship was never a rarity in the Amish community. Early settlers had been millers, tanners, brewers, and quarry operators. Others had worked as blacksmiths, carpenters, painters, furniture makers, and watch repairmen. By reviving, expanding, and mechanizing their industries, today no more than 6 percent of married men work for non-Amish employers and 75 percent still work at home, either on the land or in the farm shop or store. Some 13 percent of married Amishmen are carpenters, working together in mobile crews. Although few Amish industries have more than fifteen employees, several industries are multimillion dollar enterprises.

An Amishman calls this successful transition

a sharp turn toward home, that is back to an Anabaptist culture. Many of these shops are erected on the farm or adjacent to it. They provide the off-farm worker a job at home with or near his family, self-dependent, self-supporting, making, repairing, or selling a product that he knows is useful, one which he has a right to be proud of.[13]

CAN THIS BE PARADISE?

Everyone has a different vision of heaven, but the typical picture is of a pleasure garden. What were the pleasures in the original Eden? Besides the enjoyment of God's company, they were relatively few: the beauty of nature, the companionship of animals, human affection, the enjoyment of work, food and drink, and the simple joy of being alive. Unless you hold sex to be the original sin, there was physical love as well.

Clearly, in the biblical paradise, there were no modern movies, fashions, television, computers, automobiles, CDs, video games, telephones, electricity, restaurants, or resorts.

A case can be made that the Amish have created a working paradise along the original lines of our first parents. As Kraybill notes, they have genuine social security, the benefit of belonging, the security of family, the reward of identity, the comfort of tradition, a sure sense of meaning, as well as peace, permanence, affection, friendship, simple but rich pleasures, all tied to nature and immersed in the presence of God, who is their present and future hope.

Unlike the outside society, the Amish paradise has no crime, violence, poverty, divorce, addiction, or alienation. It is an environmentalist's dream, free of exhaust fumes, water pollution, and waste. Best of all, perhaps, it is a way of living that does not feed on ambition, competition, and anxiety.

But the costs are harsh. There is little privacy and even less individuality. Arguably, Catholic nuns enjoy more freedom in the cloister than Amish women find in their families. Adolescent males may flirt with the outside world before choosing to be baptized, but Amish girls lack alternative futures and are virtual prisoners in a patriarchal society. Moreover, there are serious problems with isolation. The last polio outbreaks in America occurred in Amish settlements in four states as recently as the 1970s.

Despite the quaintness that attracts tourists to sample the Amish way of life, it is a closed society.

Chapter 5

The Shakers: Sharing Simple Gifts

And when we find ourselves in the place just right,
'twill be in the valley of love and delight.

Shaker song, eighteenth century

For a disconnected society choked on complexity and striving, the Shakers offer the example of an alternative way of simple yet abundant living. Long before woman suffrage and civil rights, the Shakers were completely egalitarian, with women sharing leadership and responsibility with the men, and all races welcomed in fellowship. There were no "minorities" in the Shaker version of heaven on earth.

Although they labored in silence, they were exuberant in their enjoyments, inventive in their industry, and utilitarian in their daily living, leaving a legacy of functional beauty to this day in their crafts and inventions.

The Shakers were masters of cooperative self-sufficiency and inventiveness. They offer lessons in the nurturing of community, practical organization, mutual respect, and reciprocal responsibility that might enrich American society today.

At their peak in the 1840s, the Shakers consisted of as many as 6,000 individuals living in sixty separate communities spreading from Maine to Indiana. Despite the burdens of celibacy and common ownership of property, the sect flourished longer than any other utopian community that accepted men, women, and children alike. The cloister persists, of course, but only as same-sex communities of adult monks or nuns.

Although the Shakers were founded in England, they flourished in New York and New England after the initial migration in 1774. Their founder was an illiterate but Gospel-wise woman, Ann Lee, whose views on child-bearing were doubtless influenced by difficult pregnancies and the death of her four children in infancy and early childhood. Even among religious sects founded by women, the Shakers were unique in giving their female members equal empowerment with men.

The community's official name was the United Society of Believers in Christ's Second Appearing—suggesting its millenial outlook. Believing they were already living in the "last times" anticipated in Scripture, they patterned their lives on earth as they conceived the saints to live in heaven. They consciously emulated the primitive Christian community by dispensing with private property and marriage in anticipation of the imminent return of Christ and the end of the world.

Over time, some Shakers came to believe that Jesus had returned in the person of Ann Lee herself, although she expressed no such pretensions. Nevertheless, God, in the Shaker's view, was both masculine and feminine. Celibacy freed women from the burdens and dangers associated with child-bearing and enabled them to participate in the community's leadership on an equal footing with men.

That leadership was highly authoritarian, so much so that critics reviled the Shaker hierarchy as despotic and even papist. As in the monastic cloister, every aspect of Shaker's life from sunrise to sunset was regulated. In principle, men and women were equally qualified to do the same tasks, but in practice men worked in the shops and fields, leaving women to domestic chores. Visitors remarked that Shaker women appeared less healthy and happy for their self-confinement to repetitive indoor tasks.

DAILY LIVING

Except at worship, Shaker men and women were segregated, and close personal relationships between the sexes were denied in favor of loyalty and affection for the community, which stood in the place of God. Despite these restrictions, whole families—husband, wife, and children—were attracted to the Shaker communities, freely ceasing sexual relations and rejecting personal possessions as the price of allegiance to the larger community of faith.

To be sure, there was both economic and emotional security and support in such well-regulated communal living. Living in community, farmers and craftsmen were insulated from the vagaries of the seasons and the marketplace. When ill, they were cared for. When old, they were secure. The ignorant were educated.

With everyone at work—women as well as men, blacks and Native Americans as well as whites, children as well as adults—the communities were productive, and no one was poor or isolated. Shaker farms produced more than enough to sustain the members, with surpluses sold to outsiders. Shaker ingenuity created tools, implements, and crafts that were prized as commercial products.

Had not the members deliberately chosen such a simple lifestyle, many Shaker communities would have been deemed prosperous. When I published my first book, *Growing in Faith*, I chose the Shaker "Tree of Life" for its dustcover. Borrowed from the biblical Garden of Eden, its branches rich with fruit, the tree was a symbol of the Shakers' spiritual and physical abundance, of their heaven on earth, the eternal church. Their best-known hymn, "Simple Gifts," is lyrical rather than austere. Shakers prized simplicity not as denial but as a gift.

Although they were successful in forming self-sustaining economic units, Shaker leaders did not consider themselves to be social reformers. Their intent was wholly religious—to live in such a way that would achieve the Kingdom of God on earth. Historian Lawrence Foster explains their motivation:

Only by giving up all carnal propensities—including sexual intercourse and close family attachments—and devoting oneself to the worship of God within a supportive communal setting could salvation ultimately be achieved.[1]

Beyond these inflexible commitments, Shakers' theory and practice was subject to development. Rather than deifying their founder, Shakers affirmed that they merely prized her principles. In the old Christian tradition, male celibacy was often prompted by misogyny, with Adam's descendants rejecting the daughters of Eve as temptresses. By contrast, Shaker women were both revered and liberated from the burdens of child-bearing, while Shaker men freely exchanged the pleasures of the flesh for the physical and emotional support of the community.

SIMPLE GIFTS

Shakers originated as a small branch of radical English Quakers, who came to be known as the "Shaking Quakers," because they borrowed the French Camisards' ritual worship of shaking, shouting, dancing, whirling, and singing in strange tongues.

Although Ann Lee's husband accompanied her to America and supported her utopian ideals, he continued to insist on a normal marriage. But Ann was persuaded by a vision that sexual intercourse between Adam and Eve had accounted for the Fall of Man and ushered sin into the world. Nevertheless, she broke from her husband reluctantly, acknowledging that he "was very kind, according to his nature; he would have been willing to pass through a flaming fire for my sake if I would but live in the flesh with him, which I refused to do."[2]

Once free, Ann joined eight of her followers, settling near Albany, New York. For six years, the little band survived on subsistence farming while they spread their gospel. Their fortunes changed for the better when a popular Baptist preacher, Joseph Meacham, converted to Ann's faith along with his many followers. In the two years after 1781, the Shakers attracted thousands of converts in southern New England, including Free Will Baptists and many teenagers.

But the Shakers' aggressive proselytizing prompted persecution by mobs, who physically abused Ann Lee and her brother, both of whom died only a decade after arriving in America. Still, Ann's premature demise did nothing to stem the Shakers' growth.

Key to Shaker conversion was initial repentance and confession of sins to elders of the same sex and continuing acknowledgement of personal failings to the community. Confession proved to be less onerous than one might imagine, being a reminder of the convert's personal commitment to God and the community. If we are to believe the accounts of Shakers, the practice of confession was more therapeutic than intimidating, affording them the opportunity to shake off the inadequacies of their former lives.

On a visit to America, Charles Dickens sought out the Shakers and found them "grim." Later he wrote that the elder who greeted him was "a sort of grim goblin." Sociologist Rosabeth Moss Kanter acknowledges that "few utopian groups allow the luxury of laughing at themselves, although some share laughter and joy in other ways."[3] To be sure, there was nothing austere about Shakers' worship and the ecstatic dancing that gave the sect its name. In their nightly rituals, the celibate communities exchanged "gifts" of kisses and hugs. A contemporary journal noted:

We sang several songs on our knees, for we have become so used to standing on our knees that it is almost as natural for us as it is to stand on our feet....Then Elder Brother said, let us arise from our knees and greet each other with a kiss of charity, then we may be dismissed. So we all went to hugging and kissing, and loved a heap....It appeared to me that the heavens were opened and I was worshipping with the Angelic host. Some times the Brethren and Sisters were passing and repassing each other—sometimes hugging and kissing the sweetest kisses that I ever tasted, for we felt love enough to eat one another up....Sometimes the Brethren and Sisters would follow each other around and around, sometimes they would have hold of hands, three and four and sometimes a dozen in a ring, waving up and down.[4]

But during the working day, the contemporary journalist Charles Nordhoff noted,

an eternal Sabbath stillness reigns in a Shaker family—there being no noise or confusion, or hum of busy industry at any time, although they are a most industrious people.[5]

On the whole, Shakers shunned instrumental music, but all were avid singers, anxious to learn new hymns, which they professed to receive from the spirit world. Like the Quakers, they were disinclined to pray aloud, insisting that God does not need spoken words but reads men's minds and hearts. Moreover, they preferred inspiration to Bible reading.

Their physical worship was intended to emulate King David's dancing before the Ark of the Covenant. It began with marching in time to a lively hymn, then dancing in a kind of shuffle. Nordhoff noted:

Occasionally one of the members, more deeply moved than the rest, or perhaps in some tribulation of soul, asks the prayers of the others; or one comes to the front, and, bowing before the elder and eldress, begins to whirl, which is sometimes continued for a considerable time, and is a remarkable performance.... All the movements are performed with much precision and in exact order; their tunes are usually in quick time, and the singers keep time admirably.[6]

CONVERSION

Although they were wholly dependent for survival on attracting converts, the Shakers were more realistic than most utopian communities in rejecting prospects who were likely to be less than wholehearted about embracing the community as their permanent family. Prospective members were housed apart from the community, but admitted to all religious meetings and informed of Shaker beliefs and obligations.

To be admitted to the family, a convert had first to set his or her affairs in order, leaving no debts or obligations behind. A husband or wife, entering separately, required explicit spousal consent. Children also had to be provided for, either outside or within the community, before their father or mother could join.

If the converts possessed property, it was ceded permanently to the community; still, wealth made little difference. The Shakers unhesitatingly accepted devout men, women, and children who owned nothing more than the clothes on their backs. The single demand on which the community required satisfaction was the answer to the question: "Are you sick of sin, and do you want salvation from it?"

A comprehensive confession of the sins of one's entire past life to two elders of the convert's own sex was the expected response to that question. Confession and repentance was held by Elder George Albert Momas to be "the door of hope to the soul...which every sin-sick soul seizes with avidity, as being far more comforting than embarrassing." Shakers acknowledged that repentance was the work of a lifetime, "but upon this, more than upon aught else, depends their success as permanent and happy members," Momas noted. "Those who choose to use deceit, often do so, but *never* make reliable members....If *we* do not detect their insincerity, God does..."[7]

Originally, the Shakers attracted many veterans of the American Revolution. Once members, they ceased drawing on their service pensions. When the traditionally pacifist Shakers were threatened by the military draft during the Civil War, they argued with Abraham Lincoln that they had already saved the U.S. Treasury over half a million dollars due them in pensions and should be spared.

Initially, Shaker communities welcomed children, but experience proved that, once they attained adulthood, they tended to drift away. "When men or women come to us at the age of twenty-one or twenty-two, then they make the best Shakers," Elder Frederick opined.

The society then gets the man's or woman's best energies, and experience shows us that they have then had enough of the world to satisfy their curiosity and make them restful. Of course, we like to keep up our numbers; but of course we do not sacrifice our principles.[8]

Nordhoff noted that Shaker life had no charm for the vain, idle, or comfort-loving. "If one comes with low motives," Elder Frederick noted, "he will not be comfortable with us and will presently go away; if he is sincere he may yet be here a year or two before he finds himself in his right place; but if he has the true vocation he will gradually work in with us."[9]

Converts came in greatest number following the religious revivals that swept across the East and Middle West in the first half of the nineteenth century. Shakers drew their members from all denominations except the Roman Catholic. Baptists, Methodists, Presbyterians, and Adventists were the most prominent sources, and even Jews became Shakers. Black and Native Americans were as welcome as whites.

ECONOMY

Each community was founded on agriculture. As they prospered, Shakers tended to purchase more land. Farm life, with its simple labors and manners, was held to be healthy for both body and spirit. They proved to be inventive farmers, producing implements they used themselves and manufactured for others, typically without patent. These included the screw propeller, Babbit metal (an alloy for lining bearings), a rotary harrow, an automatic spring, a turbine waterwheel, a threshing machine, the circular saw, and the common clothespin. Moreover, Shakers were the first Americans to pack and market seeds, and, at their height, were the largest producers of herbal medicines in America.

The combination of simple living and celibacy was credited with ensuring the typical Shaker's long life and excellent health. When the community in Mount Lebanon, New York, constructed a hospital for its elderly and disabled members, the facility long stood empty. "Better empty than full," an aged member told Nordhoff. Elder Frederick added that "no man who lives as we do has a right to be ill before he is 60; if he suffers from disease before that he is in fault."[10]

In mid-nineteenth century, the New York legislature, alarmed at the expansion of Shaker farms, introduced a bill to limit their growth as well as the number of young apprentices the communities could hire to tend them. When the Shakers unexpectedly agreed to the terms of the proposed law, it was dropped. By then, the prosperous communities agreed that they were putting undue pressure on themselves to accept less-than-ideal young converts to cultivate the additional properties.

The communities favored being wholly self-sustaining, producing all their needs, but in time realized that they could buy cloth more cheaply than they could manufacture on their own hand looms. But they designed and manufactured their own furniture, copies of which are in demand to the present day.

Shaker furniture is noted for its lack of decoration and its fidelity to materials. To make a thing well was, according to the Shaker way of thinking, an act of prayer. They anticipated functionalism in both construction and furnishings, holding that a thing's appearance should follow on its intended use. They rejected European-inspired decoration in favor of practical austerity.

Shaker chairs were both sturdy and light, made of common pine or other locally available wood, and designed to be hung on wall pegs when floors were cleaned or the space needed for worship.

Although a Shaker village might have a total of some hundreds of members, it was divided into families consisting of from thirty to eighty men and women, plus children apprenticed to the society, living in one large house, whose upstairs rooms each accommodated from four to eight persons. A wide hall separated the men's and women's dormitories. Each room had a cot and chair for each resident, plus a desk, washing materials, a small mirror, and a stove for heating. Small home-made carpets in pale colors adorned the floors.

The floors of corridors and public rooms were kept clean and highly polished. There was neither clutter nor dust. Nordhoff remarked that the absence of pictures on Shaker walls reflected not only the believers' disdain for ornament but for anything that might attract dust. The ground floor contained kitchen, pantry, storerooms, and the common dining hall, which could be converted for meetings and worship. Outbuildings were dedicated to tailoring, basket and broom-making, carpentry, laundry, and tools, plus the storage of wood, fruits, and vegetables. Besides stables, there were often machine shops and sawmills.

DAILY LIVING

The Shaker day began at 4:30 a.m. and ended at 9 p.m. in summer, 5 a.m.–9:30 p.m. in winter. Meals were at 6 a.m., noon, and 6 p.m. On rising, members folded and aired their bedclothing, washed themselves, remade their beds, and cleaned their rooms. Each male member was assigned a "sister" to care for his clothing, laundry, and general neatness. She was required to reprove him, if need be, for any slovenly habits. Women prepared the meals, kitchen crews rotating each month. Younger sisters washed and ironed.

Pork was prohibited, and many Shakers were vegetarians and even vegans, disdaining any food produced by animals, including milk, butter, and eggs. Fruit from the community's own orchards and gardens was consumed at every meal. At harvest time, the entire male community dropped usual tasks to help in the fields. The sisters' outdoor work was typically limited to gathering fruit and vegetables for the common table.

Evenings were devoted to wholesome diversions, including the singing of hymns. Nordhoff noted that some sort of family meeting was held after dinner every evening. On Mondays at Mount Lebanon, for example, the community gathered to hear articles read from newspapers. Crime reports were skipped-over. Communications from other Shaker communities were also shared. Tuesday evening was given over to singing and marching, Wednesday to conversation. Thursday night was devoted to a "laboring meeting"—a religious service where members "labored to get good." Friday evening was occupied by the learning of new songs, and Saturday evening to worship. On Sunday evenings, male and female members were permitted to visit one anothers' rooms by invitation, but not privately. Usually, three or four sisters would join a like number of brothers in their room to sing and converse.

Throughout the long days, Shakers were composed and content but never idle. Although they often purchased commercial cloth, they made their own clothing. They also made shoes, constructed their own buildings, and furnished them. Their barns were known for being cleaner than most Americans' houses. The men cut firewood by power saw, storing it in great rooms where it dried. "In their farming operations," Nordhoff noted, "they spare no pains; but, working slowly year after year, redeem the soil, clear it of stones, and have clean tillage. They are fond of such minute and careful culture as is required in raising garden seeds. They keep fine stock, and their barns are usually admirably arranged to save labor."[11]

When prosperous Shaker families purchased outlying farms, they hired laborers to till the fields and built comfortable homes for these non-Shakers, thereby gaining the reputation for being honest and fair in their dealings with the world of commerce.

They dressed simply in the manner of the time. Men wore broad stiff-brimmed felt hats and long light blue coats. Women wore long-pleated gowns and a cap that completely covered their hair. Outdoors the sisters added a deep sun-bonnet. Although members dressed in similar fashion, there was no Shaker uniform. They chose convenience and simplicity over fashion, and adapted clothing to the seasons.

GROWTH AND TRIALS

Within three years of Ann Lee's death, Joseph Meacham assumed her authority over the movement, affirming Christian communism, and ensuring an equal leadership role for women. At the outset, many Shakers, although venerating their female founder, resisted female leadership as contrary to Christian tradition. Meacham underscored his intentions by declaring women's role to have been given him by divine revelation, and he appointed Lucy Wright as his coequal leader.

Shaker men continued for a time to resist female authority, and Shaker women were reluctant to assume traditional male responsibilities. When Meacham died in 1796, a so-called "great apostasy" ensued as Lucy Wright survived as leader and male members departed. But in the two-century history of the Shakers, there was no successful schism, probably because the system of governance was so clear and hierarchical. Historian Lawrence Foster notes that

supreme authority was vested in the head ministry at New Lebanon, New York, usually four in number, two of each sex. The head figure of this ministry had the authority, tempered only by the sentiments of the membership, to appoint or replace the other three members, and with them, all the leadership of the various Shaker communities.[12]

It was celibacy that enabled Shaker women to become community leaders. A celibate lifestyle permitted women to ignore St. Paul's admonitions to wives to be subject to their husbands and to keep silent in worship. Like nuns, Shaker women considered themselves to be married to Christ and subject only to God and the needs of the Shaker family. Paul, they noted, was himself celibate, and they accepted his teaching that there is neither male nor female in the Lord.

At the outset of the nineteenth century, Shakerism was thoroughly institutionalized and growing as a movement. By 1820, seven new communities were established in Ohio, Kentucky, and Indiana, nearly doubling the numbers of the faithful. The missionary expansion was fueled by Shaker writing and publication, forcing the adherents to justify to others the unusual tenets of their faith. In defense of celibacy, they quoted God's curse upon Eve:

I will greatly increase your pains in childbearing; with pain you will give birth to children. Your desire will be for your husband, and he will rule over you. (Genesis 3:16)

Celibacy, it seemed clear to them, was the antidote to the creator's curse and to the fallen state of men and women alike, who had sinned through lust. If sex could be controlled, Shakers believed, all social problems could be alleviated. Except perhaps in their earliest fervor, they did not regard married sex as actually sinful, but rather as a distraction from a godly life.

Beginning in 1837 and lasting a decade, Shakers experienced a rash of what they considered spiritual manifestations, chiefly among women and youths, who became subject to hearing voices, seeing visions, speaking in tongues, entering trances, and manifesting divine possession by violent shaking and ecstatic dancing. Initially, these displays revived the brothers' and sisters' spiritual commitment, but over time became disruptive of authority, prompting a loss of teenage females to the society and promulgation of the strict Millennial Laws of 1845, which further defined acceptable Shaker behavior.

The reforms came none too soon. Young Shaker mediums had persuaded themselves that they were delivering revelations not only from Jesus, St. Paul, Mary Magdalene, and the saints, but from Christopher Columbus, George Washington, Napoleon, and the queens Elizabeth and Isabella. The crackdown in discipline took a humorous turn as elders attempted to micromanage the members' lives. For example, one of the Millennial Laws specified that "Sisters must not mend, nor set buttons on brethren's clothes while they still have them on."

THE SHAKER APPEAL

It is difficult to adequately portray the almost manic-depressive religious fervor that swept across the young nation, offering high hopes to tens of thousands of seekers after salvation, only to dash them as the revivals receded. As we will see, a bewildered Joseph Smith would reject revivalism altogether in favor of a new revelation, Mormonism, and a new community, the Latter-day Saints. By contrast, the Shakers, carried along by the spirit of inspiration, chose to institutionalize the godly life, providing stable and safe communities in which to work out one's salvation.

Although they lived in anticipation of Christ's Second Coming, the Shakers did not attempt to predict its date. Indeed, most members were inclined to believe that Ann Lee had already ushered in the final times mentioned in Scripture. The many disciples of William Miller became disillusioned when the popular preacher's prediction of Jesus' return in 1843 or 1844 failed. Their sorrow became known as the Great Disappointment. The most prominent Millerite publicist, Enoch Jacobs, converted briefly to Shakerism and brought many disaffected Millerites with him, among them Henry B. Bear, who appealed, "O come and be gathered...I know there can be no happiness in being thus scattered."[13]

Shaker theology enjoyed the dual appeal of being both strict and unorthodox, settled and enthusiastic. Its belief in continuing revelation opened the door for all kinds of seekers who were unhappy with traditional Christian churches and the dour Calvinism that was the Puritans' legacy. When, in 1808, free-thinking Thomas Jefferson was sent a copy of the

Shakers' *Testimony of Christ's Second Appearing,* he called it the best church history he had ever come across, and professed to have read it nine times over.

Shakers rejected the traditional Trinitarian God as exclusively masculine, insisting that divinity, like creation, combines both masculine and feminine elements. Christ's first coming was as a man, Jesus. Christ's second manifestation was as a woman, Ann Lee, they believed. Their great contribution, however, was not theological, but practical—incorporating the spiritual and temporal world within working communes of men and women, effectively institutionalizing the monastic tradition of seeking salvation in community.

By 1830, the Shakers had reached their apogee as a movement, forming eighteen additional communities across New York, New England, and the Midwest. Much earlier, they were so well established that, when an epidemic of cholera hit New York City in 1803, two Shaker farms contributed thousands of dollars worth of cash, food, and livestock to feed the starving city dwellers. But the Shakers disdained city life, preferring agriculture and the relative isolation of the countryside.

A British visitor in 1867 wrote, "The people are like their village...soft in speech, demure in bearing, gentle in face; a people seeming to be at peace not only with themselves, but with nature and heaven."[14] When the Panic of 1837 threatened the American economy, adversity furthered and strengthened the spiritual lives of the Shakers.

THE STUMBLING BLOCK

Over time, however, the movement's total reliance on converting men and women to celibate lives proved to be its undoing. The former Millerite, Enoch Jacobs, was a married man. Jacobs and his wife wrestled with the demand that they renounce their relationship. He wrote to other Millerites:

I now ask if there is one Advent believer in the land who would not gladly share the peaceful home (the Shakers) enjoy were it not for the cross (celibacy)? Excuse after excuse is brought forward, while the real one is hidden. You wish to reserve the privilege of gratifying the lusts of the flesh, which you know you cannot do under any circumstances, in the dispensation in which we live, appealing to God that you do it for his glory.[15]

After a brief sojourn among them, Jacobs reluctantly left the Shakers, acknowledging that he would "rather go to hell with Electa (his wife) than live among the Shakers without her."

Over time, many of the disaffected Millerites became disenchanted with Shakerism as well. Between 1830 and the dissolution of the Shaker community at New Lebanon sixty-six years later, membership records reveal that only slightly more than one in ten converts remained in the community for the rest of their lives. As early as 1830, before the Millerite infusion, the length of time the converts remained in community was shrinking. By 1874, the society was actually advertising for members. At the turn of the twentieth century, there were but a thousand Shakers, and by the late 1970s, only a dozen female members survived in Maine and New Hampshire.

Father James Whittaker, an early Shaker Elder, predicted of the Shaker faith, "If there are but five souls among us that abide faithful, this testimony will overcome all nations." Earlier, Ann Lee herself said that "This gospel will go to the end of the world, and it will not be propagated so much by preaching, as by the good works of the people."[16]

In 1972, the Great Stone Barn at Mount Lebanon, New York, burned to the ground. The following year the cow barn at Canterbury Shaker Village was also lost to fire. Built in 1856, it was the largest barn in the state of New Hampshire.

Despite these disappointments, the Hancock Shaker Village at Pittsfield, Massachusetts, was completely restored and opened in 1968 as a museum celebrating Shaker life.

AN IMPROBABLE REVIVAL

For want of other accommodations, one spring night in 1991, eight teenage members of a rock group called "The Shakers" camped out on the grounds of the Hancock museum prior to their performance at a local school. They were amused at the coincidence of names but had no previous knowledge of Shakerism. But next morning, the six boys and two girls confessed to one another that they had received visions that transformed their lives. Calling themselves "New Shakers," the eight launched a missionary effort among teens that in four years claimed 100,000 members in communities from Seal Harbor, Maine, to La Jolla, California.

Their creed was simple: "No hate, No war, No money, No sex." By 1995, the New Shakers boasted sixty-one separate "tribes" containing as many as fifteen "families" of 128 members each. In the Hudson River hamlet they call Jerusalem West, local members live together under a translucent dome, surviving on stew and financing their lifestyle by fixing-up and selling castoff automobiles. The New Shaker motto is "Work is Play."

Like the original Shakers, they worship by dancing, sixty-four boys on one side, matched by sixty-four girls on the other, each an arm's length apart. But unlike the disciples of Ann Lee, they prefer ear-piercing rock-and-roll hymns to "Simple Gifts." What they seek in their jerking, writhing, ecstatic dancing is what they call the Gift of Seizure.

In an interview, Harry G., one of the New Shaker founders, was asked, "What's your attitude toward the Old Shakers? They died out, didn't they, for lack of recruits?"

As only the young can, Harry G. dismissed the question as irrelevant. "Everything is born and dies and gets reborn again,"[17] he replied.

Chapter 6

The Mormons: To the Promised Land

This is the place!

Brigham Young

The Mormons offer the largest single example of spiritually motivated utopian living in America today. Motivated by a faith native to the United States, they overcame persecution, assassination, and the terrors of the wilderness to create their heaven on earth in the desert. But rather than shrinking into their own enclaves, they became a vital missionary people, determined to share their vision of the best of all possible worlds.

For the edification of the larger society, the Latter-day Saints offer practical examples of community building, generosity, mutual aid, dedication to work, reverence for humanity, strength of family, responsibility, and comradeship.

A magnificent migration of 148 pioneers ended on July 24, 1847, when their leader, Brigham Young, on sighting the valley of the Great Salt Lake, pronounced that this is where his Latter-day Saints would build their Zion. By any estimation, it was a journey of faith unmatched since the Israelites' exodus from Egypt to the Promised Land. It was repeated in 1856 when converts, pulling handcarts, trekked from Iowa City to the New Jerusalem.

To this day, Utah and its adjacent states constitute a uniquely American empire of faith, the most conspicuous illustration on our continent of the conversion of religious vision into brick-and-mortar reality. Nowhere else in America does a single faith so dominate daily living. And the Mormon migration has never ended. Today no community of any size in the United States lacks a local church of the denomination.

There are already more than five million Latter-day Saints in the United States, and the faith is spreading, thanks to 60,000 missionaries in 160 nations. In the past thirty years, its numbers worldwide increased nearly four-fold to over eleven million. The majority are first-generation converts.

Without consulting them, Mormons have also baptized by proxy some 200 million deceased persons, among them the Buddha, the Popes, Shakespeare, Einstein, and even Elvis Presley. During the 1990s, over Jewish objections, attempts were made to baptize victims of the Holocaust.

Once despised, persecuted, and exiled by their neighbors, Mormons have long since become respected members of the civic and business community everywhere—plain-spoken, sober-minded, generous, hard working, and disciplined. As a people they have thrived economically. The church itself has assets estimated by *Time* at $30 billion. It owns lands in the continental United States equivalent to the state of Delaware.

In February 2002, the world came to the Mormon paradise—site of the Winter Olympic games. Despite downplaying of Mormon culture by the (ex-Mormon) mayor of Salt Lake City, the foreign press was fascinated by the uniquely American faith. Latter-day Saints church leaders were content to inform rather than proselytize them—providing 4,000 clean-cut volunteers dressed in dark suits and simple dresses to serve as aides.

Mitt Romney, head of the Salt Lake Organizing Committee, (later to become governor of Massachusetts) is a Mormon bishop. Since Utah's governor, congressional delegation, Olympic organizing committee, and the vast majority of local leaders are also Mormons, faith could not help but infect the games. For ten nights during the course of the competition, the 21,000 seat conference center in Salt Lake City's Temple Square presented a song-and-dance extravaganza entitled "Light of the World." Two of the most identifiable Mormons in American entertainment, Donny and Marie Osmond, provided hourly updates on the Olympic competition over a local TV station.

MORMON ORIGINS

In 1827, Joseph Smith, Jr., son of a poor New England farmer, claimed to have been directed by an angel, Moroni, to unearth golden plates on which were inscribed new divine revelations. With the aid of special stones, the young seeker translated what would become *The Book of Mormon,* the scriptures of his sect. Three years later, at the age of twenty-six, he founded the Church of Jesus Christ of Latter-day Saints.

Smith was raised in a part of upstate New York known as the "burned-over district" for the heat of its religious ferment. Distressed by the conflicts among faiths, the boy "often said to myself, what is to be done? Who of all these parties be right? or are they all wrong together?" He found reassurance in the Epistle of St. James, which stated, "If...any of you does not know how to meet any particular problem, he has only to ask God—who gives generously to all men without making them feel guilty—and he may be quite sure that the necessary wisdom will be given him."[1]

In 1820, the 14-year-old Smith entered a forest grove to meditate on these words and reported an encounter with two heavenly visitors, the Father and the Son, who counseled him to join no existing religious party but to await new revelations. Those inscribed on the golden plates were said by Moroni to have been compiled by Mormon, the angel's father.

Three male associates, as well as Smith's wife, Emma, testified to have handled the plates. The three, Oliver Cowdery, Martin Harris, and David Whitmer, signed an affidavit, affirming that "an angel of the Lord came down from heaven, and he brought and laid before our eyes, that we beheld and saw the plates, and the engravings thereon."[2] Later, all three witnesses issued denials, but two of them returned to the Mormon faith. Although Whitmer never returned, he insisted to the rest of his life that his original testimony was true. Once translated, Moroni returned the plates to heaven.

As Smith's following grew, his disciples established themselves in Kirtland, Ohio, and in Missouri, creating a communistic and polygamous society, the United Order of Enoch. The prophet, however, preferred cooperative society to common property. From the outset, the Saints drew the envy and enmity of their neighbors, who burned Mormon property, murdered the disciples, and tarred and feathered the prophet himself.

The Book of Mormon denounces plural marriage, and throughout Smith's life monogamy was the official teaching of the church. The prophet himself acknowledged only Emma as his spouse. She bore him nine children. However, fellow Mormons acknowledged that he was a compulsive philanderer and likely "married" as many as fifty wives in secret ceremonies—some of the women already married to disciples. In his last years, Smith averaged one new wife a month. In July, 1843 Smith made a new revelation justifying his behavior: "If any man espouse a virgin, and desire to espouse another, and the first give her assent," it is not adultery.[3]

In 1839, under persecution in Missouri, the Mormons crossed the Mississippi, settling in Commerce, Illinois, which they renamed Nauvoo. The city fast became the largest in the state with 20,000 citizens. It was dominated by a temple to the new faith. Smith became mayor and commander of the Nauvoo Legion, part of the Illinois militia.

Five years later, when Smith announced his candidacy for President of the United States, dissident disciples attacked him in print for polygamy and political ambition. The mayor ordered the press destroyed and called out his militia to put down mob violence in the aftermath. Charged with treason, Smith and his brother Hyrum were imprisoned in the Carthage city jail. Despite promises of protection by the governor, on June 27, 1844, the brothers were set upon by a mob and murdered.

TREK TO DESTINY

Brigham Young, a carpenter, joiner, painter and glazier, was forty-three when Smith died. He had already directed the Mormon migration from Missouri to Nauvoo. Now, in the face of mob pressure, he led the Mormons west out of Illinois in 1846, reaching the Missouri River that summer. In the following year, they reached the valley of the Great Salt Lake and established their Zion. Young returned to winter quarters in Nebraska later that year, and in 1847 became head of the church. Joining the next migration in 1848, he then remained in Utah for the rest of his life, making Salt Lake City the base for Mormon missions throughout the West.

Young became governor of the provisional state of Deseret in 1849. When it was declared a U.S. territory, he continued as governor, serving two terms, but was replaced in 1857 at the behest of President James Buchanan, who sent an army to ensure federal rule after complaints by the U.S. judiciary. Young never again held public office, but by dint of being president of the church effectively ruled Utah until his death in 1877.

Young was less a prophet than a tireless and effective administrator. Taking advantage of his coreligionists' isolation, he formed them into a cohesive society, encouraging education, the arts, and economic self-sufficiency. He died a wealthy man. His single most important doctrinal introduction was that of plural marriage, which he honored by becoming husband to as many as fifty-five wives.

In 1866, Young declared, "The only men who become gods, even the sons of God, are those who enter into polygamy."[4] Elsewhere in America, it was assumed that the practice of plural marriage was equivalent to sexual bondage, but most Mormon women were quick to insist that they chose such marriages freely and willingly. Young himself was arguably an early feminist, encouraging women to enter male-dominated professions such as medicine and the law. As governor, he gave Utah's women the vote—the first instance of woman suffrage in America.

During the remainder of the nineteenth century, over a thousand Mormon men were imprisoned for offenses related to polygamy. Others fled to Mexico and Canada to continue the practice. When, in 1890, the U.S. Supreme Court authorized the confiscation of Mormon property everywhere, the church's then-president experienced a new revelation that plural marriage was no longer permitted.

THE CHALLENGE OF SEXUALITY

Plural marriage had been a Mormon solution to a problem common to all utopian endeavors—how to ensure community in the presence of human sexuality, which is by nature exclusive. How can property be held in common for the good of all when couples are instinctively possessive of each other?

The cloister met the challenge by creating separate communities of men and women, with members renouncing sexual relations altogether. The Shakers also renounced sexual activity but managed to nurture an integrated community of both men and women, even adopting children of non-Shakers into their family.

The Oneida Community would take a different tack. As we shall see, it approved of free love between the sexes in the community so long as couples did not form exclusive romantic relationships. Moreover, to ensure that children were not born of these liaisons, the community mandated a form of male continence.

From the outset, Mormons were inclined to communitarianism but in practice permitted private property so long as none of the saints went in need. Through tithing and volunteerism, an extensive welfare system was created that provided for all. To its credit, the streets of Salt Lake City, unlike those of the Nation's Capital, are not strewn with beggars. The focus of Mormon life was and remains on the family, not on the individual. Marriage was first a matter of responsibility, only secondarily that of romance.

Mormons take an almost puritanical approach to sex, belying the popular image of Mormon males creating harems like sultans. Tim Heaton, who teaches demographics at Brigham Young University, points to four "Cs" of the Mormon character: chastity, conjugality, chauvinism, and children.[5] Mormon senior high school boys are seven times more likely to be virgins than their non-Mormon classmates. The virginity rate of Mormon girls the same age is three times greater than their non-Mormon peers.

The emphasis is on being married and raising a family, with the father as its head and mother staying at home to raise the children. Mormons tend to marry in their early twenties (most Americans, on average, now wed in their late twenties) and produce half again as many children as non-Mormon parents.

In pioneer times, polygamy was defended under the assumption that there was a surplus of women on the trail West to be cared for. That now appears not to have been the case. Still, plural marriage did ensure that nearly all Mormon women, including widows, were not left to fend for themselves. Moreover, unlike wives in monogamous marriages, Mormon women in the pioneer period were pregnant less often and thus less prone to death in childbirth. The birthrate in plural marriages was lower than in monogamous ones.

Moreover, polygamy was defended on the basis of the Mormons' belief that there are preexisting spirits waiting for human bodies to inhabit. It is the responsibility of parents to produce those bodies.

CLEAN LIVING

On average, Mormons live more than a decade longer than other Americans, partly because there is no poverty among them. But they are also notoriously clean-living, eschewing alcohol, tobacco, and other stimulants, including coffee and tea. Since Coca-Cola, a Mormon-dominated corporation, puts caffeine in some of its soft drinks, strict Mormons are ambivalent whether Coke is a permissible beverage.

Not only do Mormons live longer, but also they are healthier than other Americans, suffering less from heart disease and cancer.

However, they have a higher incidence of diabetes, possibly because sugar serves as a substitute for pleasures they do not permit themselves. Jell-O was voted the state's official snack food. Moreover, self-denial may lead to depression: Utah leads the nation in the use of prescription antidepressant drugs. Its citizens' reliance on Prozac is 60 percent higher than the national average.[6]

Consistent with the value they place on marriage and the family, Mormons condemn adultery and promiscuity. They also frown on divorce and contraception, but acknowledge both. Saints discourage the single life. They consider "pernicious" the primitive Christian notion that celibacy might be a higher spiritual state of living than marriage.

Lawrence Wright, writing in *The New Yorker*, marvels that a people so unique "are ostensibly so conventional. Mormons have managed to make themselves into an ethnic group without any of the usual markers of ethnicity—no distinctive language or accent, no special foods or music."[7]

What is distinctive is their work ethic. The state symbol is the bee—a very industrious bee—yet the Mormon quest for success appears not to be compromised by workaholism and Type A behavior, but rather marked by dedication and optimism. Professor Harold Bloom calls Mormons "perhaps the most work-addicted culture in religious history."[8] Its work ethic suits a people who believe that worldly success translates into an eternal fulfillment that is itself active. The work ethic prevalent among individual Mormons explains why the church itself operates along business lines and has so many corporate holdings.

Welfare is also a business among the Saints that follows the collectivist rule: "From each according to his ability, to each according to his needs." Saints are required to tithe between 10 and 15 percent of income and donate as many as forty hours a week as volunteers. The church sponsors perhaps the largest private welfare organization in the nation, providing not only services to the needy, but actually manufacturing food and household needs, nearly all with volunteer assistance.

On winter nights as many as 2,000 homeless sought shelter, most of them in Salt Lake City. Before the 1996 Summer Olympics, Atlanta city fathers gave that city's vagrants one-way bus tickets out of town to rid the streets of them. In Salt Lake City before the 2002 Winter Games, its mayor's spokesman said, "We're not giving bus tickets to anybody. We're giving them beds and we hope something more, like job training and transitional housing and substance abuse treatment, and we'll be doing that after the Olympics are over."[9]

MORMON MISSIONS

If the Saints' lives appear conventional, Mormon beliefs are anything but. Their insistence on being considered Christians belies their reliance on revelations beyond those contained in the Bible, and on their prophet, Joseph Smith. When I mentioned in my syndicated newspaper column that the Mormon practice of evangelizing door-to-door and two-by-two reproduces the example of the apostles, I was peppered with angry letters from Christian readers denouncing the Saints as heretics.

To be sure, the Mormons are not ecumenical. They refer to all non-Mormons (including Christians, Jews, and Muslims) as "gentiles," styling themselves as God's chosen people charged with leading all others to salvation. That said, for a people who chose geographic isolation, they are not exclusive. Indeed they are arguably the most aggressively *inclusive* religious sect in the world, literally proselytizing at every door, welcoming newcomers to the fold.

Like Quakers, Mormons have no separate paid clergy. Church officers are appointed from the membership. Still, once he reaches the age of sixteen, any Mormon boy can become a priest. Later, if he goes on mission, he graduates to the position of "elder." Those fresh-faced, earnest young men who appear at your door are typically giving two years of their lives to this lonely work.

Olympic organizer and Massachusetts governor Mitt Romney, son of a three-term Michigan governor, served as a young man on missions in Paris and Bordeaux. He laughs at his attempts to convert the French to a religion that would require them to give up their wine. But Romney is philosophical: "It was good training for how life works....Rejection of one kind or another is going to be an important part of everyone's life."[10]

Fifteen centers around the world train the young missionaries to speak one of fifty foreign languages. Once at their destinations, they devote six days a week to knocking on doors and living a spartan existence. Homesickness is not tolerated on mission. The young men can phone home only on Christmas and Mother's day and write but once a week. They may not date, watch television, or listen to the radio.

For this effort, the average missionary makes fewer than five converts. No matter, explains Brigham Young University professor Ronald W. Walker: "The kids go out and may convert a few here and there, but, more important, they convert themselves."[11] As ever, religion thrives in adversity.

THE MORMON FAITH

Mainstream Christians do not aspire to be god-like, but only to be saved. By contrast, Mormons believe that every person is potentially divine, and that God himself was formerly human. "As man is now, God once was; as God now is, man may be," is their ambitious belief. Indeed, they believe God himself was once mortal, with a wife and children. The current president of the Latter-day Saint Church, nonagenarian Gordon B. Hinkley, says, "We believe in eternal progression," evolving toward divinity by following Mormon discipline. "We believe that life, eternal life, is real, that it's purposeful, that it has meaning, that it can be realized."[12]

Joseph Smith was born in a time of utopian vision, when Ralph Waldo Emerson commented that every literate man had a plan for a new society in his waistcoat pocket. But Smith had more—a vast new revelation and a new reading of history on the American continent.

The Book of Mormon speaks of two antagonistic tribes of Israel, the good Nephites and evil Lamanites, who migrated to the North America, and were visited by the resurrected Jesus, who temporarily reconciled them. But four centuries later, the Lamanites reverted to their old ways and murdered the Nephite leader, Mormon, and hundreds of thousands of his disciples. Moroni survived to record the tale on the golden plates, which he directed Smith to unearth and translate.

There is no anthropological or archeological evidence to point to the existence of these pre-Columbian peoples. Nevertheless, Smith's account caught the imagination of people drawn to the notion that they were mortal gods. In his vision, the Holy Land was no longer in the Middle East, but here in America. He believed the original Garden of Eden to have been near Independence, Missouri, roughly in the center of the United States.

Whereas conventional Christianity appreciates the Trinity as one God in three Persons, Mormons believe Father, Son, and Spirit to be distinct individuals. Human souls preexist their incorporation into physical bodies. People are essentially good, uncompromised by Original Sin. Mormons believe in both free will and justification by faith, but consider salvation to be a person's own responsibility, ensured by obeying the ordinances of the church. Baptism is by immersion and the laying on of hands.

The Book of Mormon portrays hellfire for the unregenerate, but Smith later described three distinct eternities: celestial, terrestrial, and telestial. In the first, faithful Mormons inherit eternal life as gods. In the second, even those who sin live on in glory. The third ("telestial") kingdom is not divine but located on another earth, serving as eternal home to liars and adulterers.

THE AMERICAN RELIGION

The great nineteenth-century explorer Richard Burton travelled to Utah to admire the Mormon society. Russian novelist Leo Tolstoy called Mormonism "the American religion," saying he "preferred a religion which professed to have dug its sacred books out of the earth to one which pretended that they were let down from heaven."[13]

Tolstoy added:

The Mormon people teach the American religion; their principles teach the people not only of heaven, and its attendant glories, but how to live so that their social and economic relations with each other are placed on a sound basis. If the people follow the teachings of this Church, nothing can stop their progress—it will be limitless.

The editor of the (non-Mormon) Salt Lake City *Tribune* claims that "we live in a quasi theocracy. Eighty percent of officeholders are of a single party, 90 percent of a single religion, 99 percent of a single race, and 85 percent of one gender."[14] Nevertheless, the Mormon Church distances itself from politics, refusing to endorse parties or candidates. It does, however, take public positions on moral issues, such as abortion and homosexuality.

Until 1978, the church excluded male Americans of African descent from the priesthood, sensing that they might be related to the dark-skinned Lamanites who murdered Mormon. Despite that accommodation there are few black Saints. In the 1970s, the church took an aggressive stance against the proposed Equal Rights Amendment (ERA) and excommunicated the Mormon Sonia Johnson in 1979 for her activism in promoting the ERA.

Ironically, women had greater influence in Mormonism during the period of polygamy than they do today. Historian Lawrence Foster notes that

In the absence of their husbands, who could often be gone for extended periods of time, plural wives ran farms and businesses and became of necessity the acting heads of households....Plural wives could and often did cooperate with each other in handling child care and other work or in freeing an ambitious or talented wife to pursue a professional career.[15]

In recent times, Mormon women lost financial control of their Relief Society and its magazine, and have been pressed to confine their energies to family life. However, in 1990, temple rituals were quietly altered to favor women. No longer must brides pledge obedience to their husbands nor veil themselves during part of the marriage ritual. They are still excluded from the Mormon priesthood but are otherwise active in the work of the church.

THE TEST OF CHARITY

The separation of church and state in Mormon Utah could hardly be more dramatic. Salt Lake City's temple and the state Capitol are within blocks of each other, but there is no commerce between them. Mormonism respects government but believes that the less of it, the better.

As Mormon congressman Chris Cannon explains, life on earth is a time of moral testing. For the test to have any meaning, people must be free agents, not having their lives micromanaged by bureaucrats and regulated by government. The government should protect people but leave them to make their own choices.

Nowhere is separation of church and state more apparent than in education. Rather than build Mormon schools, Utah supports public education free of religious instruction. However, the church often builds classrooms adjacent to the school so that the Mormon boys and girls can learn about their faith after their regular classes end.

Because they believe in limited government, Mormons take responsibility for public welfare on themselves. It is a "faith-based initiative" run without reliance on tax dollars. Rather, Mormons fast twice a month, donating the cost of the food they would have enjoyed to a local church fund for the needy. Even a small Mormon congregation collects over $50,000 a year to aid the poor. With 3,600 congregations in Utah alone, the practice of fasting raises almost $200 million annually, almost as much as the Utah state government spends on healthcare.

Mormon charity operates free of bureaucracy. Charitable donations stay within the local congregation to be meted out by volunteers as needs arise. U.S. Senator Bob Bennett was once such a volunteer. "I could write out a check for $500 and just hand it over to someone I thought needed it,"[16] he explains.

Welfare works among Mormons without red tape because congregations are small, everyone knows everybody, and everyone trusts the volunteers. When one congregation was asked for help by an unemployed member who found a job but could not get to it, they bought her a used car. As *The Economist* marvels, "There is no sense of entitlement, so no welfare-dependency."[17]

Moreover, the church can directly provide food and jobs to the needy. It operates its own chain of supermarkets and can approve a poor family's shopping list for free groceries. It can even provide temporary jobs in its farms, canneries, and stores. The Mormon welfare system works not only because its members give up time and money, but because they know the persons in need and can help them directly.

PROSPECTS FOR THE MORMON PARADISE

Mormons, like Quakers, consider themselves a "peculiar people," set apart and distinctive, despite their fairly easy assimilation into secular society, both nationally and internationally. Just as the early Christians felt bound by their solidarity with the crucified Christ, Mormons remember their own persecution, the murder of their founder, and the occasion when the federal government dispatched an army to exterminate them. Like the Jews, they believe that there are definite costs to being a "chosen people."

Can their sense of separation and destiny be maintained when Utah's Saints constitute only 14 percent of the church's growing worldwide membership? Mormon leaders believe so, relying on discipline and organization to keep the Mormon identity distinctive. Although the church is expanding, Mormon life is largely local, familial, fraternal, intimate, and interdependent. The Saints know that they can rely on one another.

Mormonism suffers estrangement from other churches, ranging from suspicion to outright hostility, partly due to the Saints' aggressive proselytizing. Although the Catholic Church generally accepts Protestant baptisms, in 2001, the Vatican ruled that Mormon baptisms are invalid. Most Protestant denominations also demand rebaptism of converts from Mormonism. Then again, the Saints require that converts from other denominations be baptized again in the Mormon church.

The Rev. Lee Shaw, a former Mormon, is now an Episcopal priest at St. James Church in suburban Salt Lake City. He encourages Mormons who wish to join one of the more-traditional Christian denominations to approach baptism as a "healing sacrament." Saints who come to have doubts about their faith are commonly pressured by family, friends, and coworkers to remain Mormon under threat of being alienated from their families for all eternity.

In 2001, the *Salt Lake Tribune* revealed in a poll that two-thirds of Utah's citizens sensed a cultural fault between Mormons and Gentiles. The problem more likely stems from the rank-and-file members rather than from the church's leadership, which is aggressively ecumenical. As *The Economist* notes, "The real trouble comes from the bottom of the church, not the top: the conservatism of most church members and the inward-looking quality of Mormonism almost inevitably separates Mormons from others."[18]

That said, the Mormon experiment remains the most vital living expression of the urge to build heaven on earth.

Chapter 7

The Oneida Community: Love One Another

It is hell behind us, and heaven before us, and a necessity that we should march![1]

John Humphrey Noyes

Oneida stands out among successful utopian experiments in America because of its members' conviction that lasting community requires that men and women renounce emotional ties to one another in favor of being wed to the group.

In practice, group marriage at Oneida did not promote promiscuity among its members, and in its earliest decades actually contributed to a sense of responsibility and love for the community. Only later did Oneida's restrictions on emotional attachments between men, women, and children prove unworkable.

Oneida's lingering legacy to American society rests in its example of practical social organization, interdependence, mutual care and respect, cooperative labor, industry, generosity, affection, reverence, and reciprocity. Oneida became affluent because its ethical business practices enhanced commitment to community.

Utopian movements grapple with three fundamental problems—authority, property, and sexuality—each potentially destructive of community. Successful faith-based communities, while participative, are nevertheless more authoritarian and disciplined than secular society.

As for wealth, tight-knit communities favor community property or at least an equitable sharing of goods to members.

Sexuality is not so easily accommodated, because couples and their offspring are societies unto themselves. The intimacy of lovers, being exclusive, compromises their total commitment to the community. If, as Jesus noted, there is no marriage or marrying in heaven, then heaven has avoided the problem altogether. But sexuality has to be confronted in any effort to build heaven on earth.

The cloister dispensed with the problem by organizing monasteries as single sex, celibate communities. Shakers combined the sexes in community but allowed neither sexual nor emotional pairings among members. The Mormons embraced marriage but kept it from being exclusive through polygamy. Theoretically, no Mormon woman would have to live without spousal support.

Reformer John Humphrey Noyes rejected these solutions, arguing that the sexual instinct is possessive and that lovers and spouses regard each other as exclusive property. There can be no true community, he reasoned, as long as members form private bonds from which others are excluded. His radical solution was to form a loving community in which sexual and emotional exclusivity was prohibited. At Oneida, New York, given permission, any member could mate with any other so long as they avoided emotional attachment.

Noyes called his innovation "complex marriage," an arrangement whereby everyone at Oneida was in essence married to everyone else. Critics called it free love. It was clearly an experiment in group marriage, and it persisted, as the community thrived economically, for three decades beginning in 1848.

In practice, complex marriage was too restricted to qualify as free love. At Oneida, sexual suitors required not only permission of the prospective partner, but also were required to apply through a third party. Pregnancy was to be avoided by means of "male continence," not only requiring the male to withdraw before emission, but also to avoid climax altogether. Young male members were taught this control by older women beyond their childbearing years, leaving the more mature and disciplined brothers access to the fertile young sisters.

It was Noyes' intention to improve relations between the sexes. Spared pregnancy, women took their place as equals in community. When children were conceived, either accidentally or occasionally as experiments in eugenics, they were not considered offspring of the birth mother, but rather schooled and nurtured by the whole community.

Noyes, however, was no feminist, holding rather that women stood in a relationship of cooperative subordination to men. He required Oneida women, not without their complaint, to wear bloomers rather than feminine dress. The reformer sought successfully to "crucify the dress spirit" at Oneida, in hopes of creating the ideal woman: "what she ought to be, a *female man*."[2]

THE FOUNDER

Noyes was born in Brattleboro, Vermont, in 1811. Graduating from Dartmouth College, he initially entertained hopes of becoming a lawyer, then turned to theology, studying at Andover and later at Yale. He flirted with the notion of becoming a foreign missionary until, in New Haven in 1834, he was inspired by a revivalist preacher and, in his words, "landed in a new experience and new views of the way of salvation, which took the name of Perfectionism."[3]

Returning to Vermont, where his father was a banker, Noyes preached and printed his views. In 1838, he married Harriet A. Holton, granddaughter of a member of Congress, and a convert to his religious views. By 1847, he had no more than forty members in his own Vermont congregation, but his writings had created and nurtured small groups of Perfectionists in other states, who accepted him as their leader.

Already, in 1845, he had prepared the members of his congregation for life in community, incorporating his ideas on the relationship of men and women. The following year, when the Perfectionists attempted to form a commune, they were ejected from Putney as communists and libertines. Three years later, they joined believers of similar persuasion in Oneida, New York, and created a community on a neglected property of 40 acres that featured an unpainted frame house, and an abandoned Indian hut and saw mill. They paid $2,000 for the property but were otherwise impoverished, sleeping for a time on the hard floors of the garret.

Despite their original hardships, the Perfectionists' way of life soon attracted others. In 1849, a small society was formed in Brooklyn, New York, which became the center for the community's publication. The following year, another group formed in Wallingford, Connecticut, and held its property in common with Oneida.

Despite Oneida's initial poverty, the community soon thrived. Noyes' earliest followers were New England farmers, most of whom contributed some cash or property to the society. Noyes and a few others contributed several thousand of dollars each. Over the course of the next eight years, they attracted over $100,000 from members, converts, and the community's businesses.

Even during their early penury, the Perfectionists published a free newspaper and maintained a printing press. At first they concentrated on farming at Oneida, but quickly had the saw mill operating at a profit, and constructed a blacksmith shop for the making of traps, which, because of their craftsmanship, were widely in demand. Over time the Perfectionists, like the Shakers, began inventing their own machinery, and they raised fruit, made furniture, and sold cattle.

PROFITABLE COMMUNISM

By the end of the community's first decade, it had produced a net profit of over $180,000 from agriculture and other sales, which Noyes invested in purchasing more land and manufacturing capacity. By 1874, the community possessed 654 acres of vineyards and pasture at Oneida and 240 acres of orchards and grazing land at Wallingford. Altogether their holdings were worth more than half a million dollars, and income continued from sales of traps, luggage, matchboxes, and fruit preserves. Since water power was available at Oneida, in 1866, the community added silk manufacture to its output.

In 1874, membership stood at 283 men, women, and children, roughly balanced between the sexes. Of the 219 adults, fewer than half were over the age of forty. These numbers proved insufficient to maintain production, so the community hired over 200 outside laborers. With growing prosperity, Oneida hired domestic help as well for cooking, laundry, shoe-making, and tailoring. Employees were paid good wages and provided comfortable housing. The community began to attract craftsmen and professional people—lawyers, clergymen, merchants, physicians, and teachers, strengthening the services the community could provide itself internally.

Converts came from many Protestant denominations, but there were no Catholics. During 1873 alone, the Perfectionists received over 200 applications for membership, but called a halt to growth for lack of accommodations at Oneida.

Nevertheless, the society attempted to bring outsiders to their way of thinking about social reform and the relationship of the sexes. This was done principally through publications. The Perfectionists' newspaper, the *Circular*, appeared as often as three times a week and was sent without charge to anyone who expressed interest. However, the editors were clear that anyone who could afford should pay for the publication:

Those who want it and ought to have it are divisible into three classes, viz.: 1, those who can not afford to pay two dollars; 2, those who can afford to pay *only* two dollars; and, 3, those who can afford to pay *more* than two dollars. The first ought to have it free; the second ought to pay the cost of it; and the third ought to pay enough more than the cost to make up the deficiencies of the first. This is the law of Communism. We have no means of enforcing it, and no wish to do so, except by stating it and leaving it to the good sense of those concerned.[4]

The *Circular* was "published by Communists, and for Communists." Its message was Christian, unlike the 1848 atheistic Manifesto of Marx and Engels, for readers "practically devoted to the Pentecost principle of community of property."[5]

Contemporary journalist Charles Nordhoff not only visited Oneida and interviewed Noyes, but also read the *Circular* and remarked about the bogus classified advertisements it contained, which managed to be both pious and humorous. For example:

ROOMS TO LET in the "Many Mansions" that Christ has prepared for those who love him.

MAGNIFICENT RESTAURANT!—In Mount Zion will the Lord of hosts make unto all people a feast of fat things, a feast of wines on the lees of fat things full of marrow, of wines on the lees well refined...

LEGAL NOTICE.—Notice is hereby given that all claims issued by the old firm of Moses and Law were cancelled 1800 years ago. Any requirement, therefore, to observe as a means of righteousness legal enactments bearing date prior to AD 70, is pronounced by us, on the authority of the New Testament, a fraud and imposition.

THE FAITH OF PERFECTIONISTS

Noyes' followers believed they were living in the Last Times predicted in Scripture, that the second advent of Christ had coincided with the destruction of Jerusalem in AD 70, and that the final kingdom of God began then in the heavens. They accepted the apostles and the primitive church as exponents of the eternal Gospel, and believed (in Nordhoff's words) "that a church on earth is now rising to meet the approaching kingdom in the heavens, and to become its duplicate and representative."[6]

To do so, the church must be holy and its members perfect. Noyes acknowledged that "the Gospel provides for complete salvation from sin" and this salvation is the "foundation needed by all other reforms" in society.

Noyes was careful not to claim that all Perfectionists lived up to the name he gave them. Rather,

We consider the community to be a church...a school, consisting of many classes, from those who are in the lowest degree of faith to those who have attained the condition of certain and eternal salvation from sin....A sinless life is the *standard* of the community, which all believe to be practicable, and to which all are taught to aspire.[7]

According to Noyes and his followers, perfection could not be achieved merely by rule-keeping. Rather, it was a "special phase of *religious experience,* having for its basis spiritual intercourse with God." Perfectionists, Nordhoff noted, "hold that intercourse with God may proceed so far as to destroy selfishness in the heart, and so make an end to sin."[8] To destroy selfishness, Jesus' followers must renounce their claim to personal property, including exclusive attachments to another person, either spouse or child.

The journalist remarked of these demands: "It is an extraordinary evidence of the capacity of mankind for various and extreme religious beliefs, that many men have brought their wives and young daughters into the Oneida community,"[9] freely renouncing claims to their affection. "We have got into the position of Communism," Noyes warned his followers, "where without genuine salvation from sin our passions will overwhelm us, and nothing but confusion and misery can be expected."[10]

The Perfectionists dispensed with preaching, the sacraments, and observance of the Sabbath, as well as oral or formal prayer. They read and quoted the Bible frequently. Although they believed the age of miracles to be past, they believed that sufficient faith, expressed in prayer, could engage God in restoring the sick to health.

LIFE AT ONEIDA

The community lived in a large, simple building with central heating, baths, and other conveniences common to the time. The great house boasted a library with 4,000 volumes, a parlor for visitors, editorial offices, print shop, a large hall with stage for evening gatherings and performances, and two large common rooms, surrounded by bedrooms. Older Perfectionists enjoyed small private rooms; the younger lived two to a room. Furnishings were plain but not marked by Shaker austerity.

Near the main house were offices, the community school, a lecture room and laboratory, carpentry shop, photo lab, laundry, barns, stables, a silk-dyeing facility, and a small factory where children at odd hours made boxes for the spool silk. More than a mile distant from the main complex were the community's factories—trap works, silk works, a forge, and machine shops, plus housing for thirty to forty workers. The factories had the capacity of producing 3,000 traps and more than $200,000 worth of silk-twist in a year. The farm included extensive orchards of small and large fruits. Ornamental trees surrounded the main house, providing popular picnic grounds not only for the members but also for visiting groups.

Life and work at Oneida was highly organized. Administration was divided among twenty-one standing committees, responsible for a range of interests from finance to haircutting to amusements. These were policy-making groups. In addition, there were forty-eight departments responsible for the community's actual operations. They ranged from publication to business, manufacture, farming, clothing, medical and dental service, housekeeping, and even maintaining the community's clocks.

What appears to be a management nightmare was actually very efficient. Everyone in the community was involved in its governance and operations and had clear responsibilities. Everyone knew who was in charge of what. Business meetings were held every Sunday to assess the community's progress and to recommend any adjustments. Unanimous or at least general agreement was required to take any action. An oversight committee made committee assignments, usually lasting a year, but could change a member's employment at any time. An information board posted near the library indicated where any member could be located that day.

The Perfectionists' tastes and abilities were honored in assigning work. Disagreeable tasks were assigned on a rotating basis so no one was burdened by them for a longtime. As it became more prosperous, the community was able to hire outside help for jobs that were laborious or drudgery.

As the community thrived, its work-day shrank. Members rose anywhere from 5 to 7:30 a.m. depending on their assignments, and retired as early as 8:30 or as late as 10:30 p.m. Children could sleep as late as they wished. During Nordoff's visit to Oneida, meals were at 8 a.m. and 3 p.m., but the number and hours of meals were subject to change. One member acknowledged, "We used to eat three meals a day—now we eat but two; but we may be eating five six months from now."[11]

Meat was served not more than twice a week, the members' diet consisting mostly of fruit and vegetables. They drank coffee and tea but refrained from alcohol and tobacco. At dining tables seating ten to twelve persons, they served themselves from lazy susans, one of their inventions.

Perfectionists referred to one another as "Mister" and "Miss." Female members were called "Miss" even if they had borne children.

At the end of each year, the members applied to the Finance Committee for clothing they believed they would need for the coming year. The typical female member's clothing for a year, including shoes and hats, cost $33. "Minus the superfluities and waste of fashion," one member explained, "we find $33 plenty enough to keep us in good dresses, two or three for each season, summer, winter, fall, and spring."[12] One community member charged with "Incidentals" could provide breast-pins to women–the only ornament allowed to them. Men who needed a watch applied to the watch committee.

THE EDUCATION OF PERFECTIONISTS

The community's children were left to the care of their mothers until weaned, then placed in a general nursery. Nordhoff remarked on his visit that the children looked healthy and well-fed but "a little subdued and desolate, as though they missed the exclusive love and care of a father and mother," but he allowed that "this, however, may have been only fancy."[13]

Oneida's school used the Bible as a text book, but included classes in history, grammar, French, Latin, geology, and the like, not only for children during the day but for adults in the evening. From time to time, younger members were sent to outside schools and colleges to learn music, the law, medicine, engineering, architecture, and other disciplines, thereby enriching community life when they returned. Younger members, male and female alike, were encouraged to qualify for a number of tasks requiring training. Several of the Oneida girls became expert machinists.

Although most members enjoyed a better education and greater access to culture than people outside the community, and experienced greater leisure, they nevertheless struck Nordhoff as "matter of fact, with no nonsense or romance about them," and he found the female members to be "inferior to men" in education. Overall, "the predominant impression made upon me was that it was a common-place company."

After all, what else but this could be the expression of people whose lives are removed from need, and narrrowly bounded by their community; whose religious theory calls for no internal struggles, and, once within the community, very little self-denial; who are well-fed and sufficiently amused, and not overworked, and have no future to fear? The greater passions are not stirred in such a life.[14]

THE ORDEAL OF "CRITICISM"

But not all of life at Oneida was comfortable. Whereas Shakers demanded that their brothers and sisters confess their faults to one another, Perfectionists were required to listen silently to their peers' judgment of them. The institution of Criticism at Oneida called for all members to be taken to task for faults of behavior and character. The openly expressed judgment of members on members was intended to ensure that the community could govern itself without rancor or hidden agendas.

Noyes first encountered the practice as a theological student at Andover, where members of his class regularly sat in judgment of one another. The one to suffer criticism sat in silence as his confreres, in turn, reflected plainly and openly about his or her shortcomings and offenses. Noyes called it a "system of mutual criticism" that "takes the place of backbiting in ordinary society and is regarded as one of the greatest means of improvement and fellowship." At Oneida, Noyes noted:

All of the members are accustomed to voluntarily invite the benefit of this ordinance from time to time. Sometimes persons are criticized by the entire family; at other times by a committee of six, eight, twelve, or more, selected by themselves from among those best acquainted with them, and best able to do justice to their character. In these criticisms the most perfect sincerity is expected; and in practical experience it is found best for the subject to receive his criticism without replying. There is little danger that the general verdict in respect to his character will be unjust. This ordinance is far from agreeable to those whose egotism and vanity are stronger than their love of truth. It is an ordeal which reveals insincerity and selfishness; but it also often takes the form of commendation, and reveals hidden virtues as well as secret faults. It is always acceptable to those who wish to see themselves as others see them.[15]

Nordhoff was invited to attend such a session by Charles, a young man being criticized by thirty accusers, half of them women and half younger Perfectionists like himself. In turn, Charles was criticized for being spoiled by his success, for being self-important, exclusive in his friendships within the community, curt, haughty and supercilious, careless in language, critical of meals, short on table manners, irreligious, insincere, two-faced, and proud. In all, the accusations occupied half an hour, after which Noyes himself made some positive remarks about the young man's character:

Charles, as you know, is in the situation of one who is by and by to become a father. Under these circumstances, he has fallen under the too common temptation of selfish love, and a desire to wait upon and cultivate an exclusive intimacy

with the woman who is to bear a child through him. This is an insidious temptation, very apt to attack people under such circumstances; but it must nevertheless
be struggled against.[16]

Noyes publicly commended the father-to-be for the young man's decision
to isolate himself altogether from the future mother and allow another
man to become her companion. Charles Noyes noted, had taken up his
cross and volunteered to sleep with the smaller children of the community
instead, taking charge of them through the nights.

The journalist wrote of the painful session:

Every point was made; every sentence was a hit—a stab I was going to say, but as
the sufferer was a volunteer, I suppose this would be too strong a word. I could
see, however, that while Charles might be benefited by the "criticism," those
who spoke of him would perhaps also be better for their speech; for if there
had been bitterness in any of their hearts before, this was likely to be dissipated
by the free utterance.[17]

DECLINE AND DISSOLUTION

On August 28, 1879, the Oneida Community announced that it was
discontinuing the practice of complex marriage "in deference to the public sentiment which is evidently rising against it."[18] Some sixteen months
later, Oneida ceased altogether to be a community, transforming itself
into a joint-stock corporation, which persists to this day as the well-
known silversmiths.

Once before, in 1852, when the community was only four years old, it
had also suspended the practice of complex marriage, but reinstated it just
six months later. On the first occasion, it probably was outside pressure
that caused the suspension. But twenty-seven years later the decision
was made because of dissent from within the community itself.

In fact, there had been rumblings of resistance from the community's
earliest formation in Putney, Vermont. Noyes was always more interested
in spreading his ideas than in governing his community. When conflicts
arose, he typically absented himself from Oneida to concentrate on his
newspaper, living in the Brooklyn enclave most of the time in the early
years. However, when John Miller, the early resident leader at Oneida,
died in 1854, the founder was forced to return.

Nevertheless, historian Lawrence Foster notes that between 1842 and
1880 the founder "spent only about half his time at Putney and Oneida,
and he typically left at times of major stress." Foster opines that "Noyes,

deeply afraid of failure or loss of control, was hedging his bets,"[19] preferring to devote his energies to proselytism through the press rather than to
community management.

Oneida's preference for limiting its membership accounts in part
for the relative peace and prosperity the community enjoyed during its
good years. Had they recruited new members from around Oneida they
would have roused the rancor of Oneida and Madison counties. With
few people moving in or out of the community, it had the opportunity
to solidify.

The original 1852 suspension of complex marriage was undertaken
as a "fast" from conjugal freedom—a kind of self-imposed penance.
Foster believes that Noyes wished the community to concentrate on
its "severe mental and emotional problems," many of which the
historian traces to Oneida's sexual practices. Foster cites "the number
of articles appearing during this period on topics such as nervousness,
faith and unbelief, insanity, spiritualist excesses, inattention, the useless-
ness of self-condemnation, problems of insubordination, and the
like."[20]

Nevertheless, the community pulled together, reaffirmed its values, and
returned to complex marriage at the end of 1852. Noyes resumed resident
leadership in 1854, and the community's economic prosperity, plus personal loyalty to Noyes himself, largely suppressed internal dissent. But as
the original members grew older, none of the younger Perfectionists
emerged as prospective successors to Noyes, not even the founder's son
Theodore.

Oneida's younger generation, accustomed to the community's prosperity, increasingly ignored the values that the original members had carved
out of adversity. They became skeptical, secular-minded, and resistant to
the elders' authority, which they considered arbitrary and self-seeking.
Moreover, they chafed at restrictions placed by the elders on their freedom to engage in sexual relations among themselves. Because of their
youth, young men and girls were deemed to be of lower status in spiritual
perfection and expected to mate principally with older, more spiritually
mature, partners.

In sexual practice, this meant that the young men were limited to
older women, while the male elders had their choice of the young females.
A key controversy erupted over who among the men had responsibility
for initiating the community's young women into complex marriage.
To further complicate matters, Noyes initiated in 1868 a program of
practical eugenics, permitting only spiritually advanced couples to bear
children.

WAS ONEIDA A FAILURE?

In 1879, the community elected to abandon complex marriage while Oneida was still prosperous, rejecting as well the ways of the Shakers and the world, in favor of "Paul's platform, which allows marriage but prefers celibacy." In her account of the abandonment of complex marriage and subsequent breakup dissolution of the community, Constance Noyes Robertson nevertheless proclaimed the experiment a success:

...the Communists have not been the reckless bacchanalians a few have represented them. The truth is, as the world will one day see and acknowledge, that they have not been pleasure-seekers and sensualists but social architects, with high religious and moral aims, whose experiments and discoveries they have sincerely believed would prove of value to mankind.[21]

Many in the community wished to preserve it as a loose working family, but the complex venture had lost its focus. On New Year's Day 1881, the members ceased being a family and became instead commercial stockholders in the Oneida Community. Noyes died five years later. In the 1890s, the founder's son Pierrepont returned to counsel the community's descendants and transform the utopian experiment into a commercial enterprise.

Foster believes that the Oneida experiment was, on balance, a success, economically and spiritually, blending commerce with communitarianism. At a time of great divisions between the sexes and disparities in wealth in the greater society, Oneida empowered men and women alike and provided work, security, health care, and education for people of all classes and backgrounds.

The community foundered because its elders did not provide for succession in leadership. Perhaps Oneida was, in part, a victim of its own success, becoming too comfortable for its own good. The utopian spirit thrives in adversity and flags with complacency.

The practice of complex marriage, intended to bind members into one family, clearly set Oneida at odds with itself. The dispassionate affection for one's community cannot be compared with the passionate affection of lovers. Lovers are by nature possessive, but they are not exclusive in the sense of denying their need for others. Love and charity are not inimical. One kind of love complements, and even enables, the other.

Because of the bogus freedom and actual restrictions of complex marriage, sex assumed an obsessive and irritating importance at Oneida, eroding community rather than enhancing it. However wrong-headed, it was an idea intended to enable the Perfectionists to mimic heaven on earth, creating a family of mutual caring. At Oneida of a Sunday evening its members sang:

> We have built us a dome
> On our beautiful plantation,
> And we all have one home,
> And one family relation;

And men sang to the women:

> I love you, O my sister,
> But the love of God is better;
> Yes, the love of God is better—
> O the love of God is best.

To which the sisters replied:

> I love you, O my brother,
> But the love of God is better;
> Yes, the love of God is better—
> O the love of God is best.[22]

Chapter 8

The Salvation Army: Saving Body, Soul, and Spirit

No home on earth have I,
No nation owns my soul;
My dwelling-place is the Most High,
I'm under his control.

Salvationist hymn

All utopian movements aspire to create heaven on earth, but some must first confront hell. The Salvation Army dedicates itself to creating the best of all possible worlds for people who live in the worst of all possible worlds—the homeless, criminals, the unemployed, destitute, alienated, addicted, sick, and ignorant among us.

Salvationists mean to save souls for God, but from the outset, they recognized that it is complete human beings, not just their souls, that need saving. So the movement joined soup and soap to salvation. The Army offers the example that the most diminished of us are worth saving.

For most Americans, the Army appears to be a quaint welfare organization, with kettles at Christmas and resale shops for charity, with brass bands and uniformed officers like Shaw's Major Barbara. In fact, in America alone, it is a vast movement redeeming the lives of millions and a persuasive example of the good that can come from community.

General William Booth rests with his wife in an obscure North London cemetery set aside centuries ago for religious nonconformists. Were the general still with us, he would agree that Abney Park, off Church Street in Stoke Newington, is a most unattractive place in which to spend eternity. Its muddy paths are fouled with dog droppings. Tombs of the celebrated and anonymous alike are overgrown with weeds. During the blitz, German bombs not only displaced many bodies but left the cemetery chapel in ruins. Its shell is now filled with the debris of decades of neglect. Booth's unmaintained tomb is blackened and encrusted with mold.

Who could imagine that here lies the founder of one of the most successful movements ever conceived to ameliorate the human condition? To this day, Booth's Salvation Army confounds its critics and is arguably the most effective charitable organization in the United States and the world. But it is more: a noble, growing experiment in building heaven on earth.

Booth was a prophet without honor in his native England. Despite his prominence, Queen Victoria refused him an audience, and when he died in 1912 at the age of 83, he was refused burial in Westminster Abbey. Instead, he lay in state in Clapton for three days while more than 100,000 men, women, and children filed past his casket. On August 28, nearly 40,000 attended his funeral at Olympia. The burial cortege to Abney Park was followed by thousands of Salvationists and an enormous band, drawn from Salvation Army corps throughout Britain.

THE MISSION

Booth, who began his working life at age thirteen as a pawnbroker's apprentice, died as the self-commissioned commander-in-chief of a vast army. During his long life, he immersed himself in the tragic world we know from Dickens, confronting lives of unspeakable vice, poverty, hunger, violence, ignorance, and suffering for millions. To redeem the masses, he assembled a volunteer army whose only weapons were compassion and the good news of the gospel. With his wife, he not only preached the gospel in word but in deed and gave hope and sustenance to millions worldwide.

Booth was raised without religious faith by poor parents in Nottingham. In the boy's early adolescence his father died, an event that shocked William into confronting his mortality. He became a Christian without ceremony in the privacy of his own room, then, still in his teens, threw himself into the responsibilities of his new faith, preaching to the dregs of Nottingham society, and dragging the poor to the local Wesleyan chapel for worship.

At the age of twenty, Booth moved to London, working six days a week for a miserly pawnbroker, and preaching twice on Sundays at different churches. Two years later, a wealthy bootmaker, Edward Rabbits, offered to support the young man's ministry for three months at one pound a week if he would devote himself full time to Christian service.

At a party in his home, Booth's patron pressed the young preacher to read a temperance poem to his guests, many of whom were social drinkers and were vocally offended. But a young woman guest, Catherine Mumford, came to Booth's defense and made an impassioned argument for total abstinence from alcohol. She and Booth became engaged in May but waited three years to be married, during which time Booth studied for the Methodist New Connexion ministry and was ordained. Throughout his life Catherine would be his champion, companion, and most trusted advisor. Moreover, she bore him eight children over a period of a dozen years.

Booth's Methodist superiors groomed him to be a circuit minister, serving a discrete group of churches in given area. But he was at heart an evangelist and crusader, not a pastor and administrator. Catherine cautioned her husband against excessive "animal" emotion in his impassioned revivals. Yet, when a church conference proposed to limit his evangelical ministry, Catherine shouted from the gallery, "No, never!"[1] Eight weeks later, he resigned from the Methodist Church and became an independent itinerant preacher, mounting campaigns across Britain, wholly supported by the meager voluntary donations of admirers. He was only thirty-two.

GOD'S GYPSIES

It was the Booths' strategy to take religion to the masses rather than expect people to seek out the church. Officially unsponsored, the couple set about their mission on a shoestring. "We have not received as much as our travelling expenses and house rent," Catherine complained. In the early years poverty and popular rejection prompted her to feel "a good deal perplexed and tempted to mistrust." By 1863, she was pawning her jewelry. Weary of "being God's gypsy," she was nevertheless buoyed by her own success as a preacher, possibly attributable to the very novelty of a Victorian woman embracing such a public role. Handbills in the towns advertised, "Come and Hear a Woman Preach."[2]

But the Booths were ignored by respectable society, which welcomed Darwin's notion of the survival of the fittest as proof that the lower classes deserved to live in squalor. Ironically, they were also reviled by the poor, whose conditions they hoped to improve. Of his early ministry William complained:

The respectable portion of the community were too proud to enter (the chapels) and the lower orders were as positively opposed to anything of that kind as they could possibly be....Night after night I spoke to large crowds in the market square, processing through the darkest and blackest slums to the chapel into which very few would enter. So far as the door they came, but no further. It was then that I devised a special kind of meeting....To attract the people, we invited all the celebrities we knew...Men who had been remarkable in wickedness but who, we had reason to believe, were now serving God. We had a morning march, wagons in the hollow of a broken field, and meetings all day. We had great crowds of people and souls saved.[3]

With chapels largely closed to their missions, Booth took to setting up a tent. One day in July, 1865, he encountered the infamous Irish prize-fighter, Peter Monk, outside an East London pub. Nearly a half-century later Monk recalled that chance meeting:

It was the man's external appearance that attracted me. He was the finest-looking gentleman ever you saw—white-faced, dark-eyed, and a great black beard that fell over his chest. Sure, there was something strange about him that laid hold on a man.

Booth pointed at the brawler's drunken companions: "Look at those men. Look at them! There's my work looking at me." Monk agreed: "You're right, sir. Those men are forgotten, and if you can do anything for them, it would be a great work." Booth invited them all to his tent crusade.

"You're not happy, Peter Monk," Booth challenged. "You know you are not happy. You'll perish like a dog. You're living for the devil, and the devil will have you."

"Who made a prophet of you?" Monk demanded.

"My Father in heaven," Booth replied, and laid a hand on Monk's shoulder. By week's end Monk was manager of Booth's East London Mission soup kitchen.[4]

THE LONDON MISSION

When enemies collapsed Booth's tent during a packed service in East London, the evangelist was uncertain whether it could be repaired in time to continue the mission. Catherine had a better idea:

We could hire the dancing saloon in Whitechapel! It's not used on Sundays. Souls can be saved in a dancing hall as well as in a tent or church. And these people are used to going there, so it won't seem strange to them.[5]

Her husband reluctantly acquiesced, and Catherine was proved prescient, strengthening Booth's sense that they should curtail their wanderings as God's gypsies to concentrate on the capital's slums. He confessed to have

found my heart being strongly and strangely drawn out on behalf of a million people living within a mile of the tent—90 out of a hundred of whom, they told me, never heard the sound of a preacher's voice. Why go further afield for an audience? In every direction were multitudes totally ignorant of the Gospel and given up to all kinds of wickedness—infidels, drunkards, thieves, harlots, gamblers, blasphemers, and pleasure seekers without number.[6]

That Booth was a moralist is clear. But he was persuaded that those in want largely brought their own misery on themselves. He wanted to save the violent and impoverished from themselves and for God. As he and Catherine developed a following, Booth joined social service to salvation as his mission. "Soup, soap, and salvation" were just what the denizens of Dickens' slums needed. If Booth could not quite create heaven on earth, he could make life on earth less hellish, saving the unfortunate masses for the ultimate heaven.

To attract attention, he used music, spectacle, marches, and celebrities as deftly as a twenty-first-century impresario. He even turned the crowds' animosity to his own advantage, realizing that even notoriety is better than indifference.

But drawing in people for Sunday worship was insufficient when they were needy seven days a week and unprotected from violence in streets that attracted the likes of Jack the Ripper. Dickens himself published an account of a 14-year-old boy, George Ruby, who earned his living sweeping manure from the streets of London, to illustrate that poverty was both physical and spiritual:

ALDERMAN: Do you ever say your prayers?

BOY: No; never.

ALDERMAN: Do you know what prayers are?

BOY: No.

ALDERMAN: Do you know what God is?

BOY: No.

ALDERMAN: Do you know what the Devil is?

BOY: No. I've heard of the Devil, but I don't know him.

ALDERMAN: What do you know, my poor fellow?

BOY: I knows how to sweep the crossing.

ALDERMAN: And that's all.

BOY: That's all. I sweeps the crossing.[7]

THE PEOPLE'S MISSION

In his own magazine, the *East London Evangelist,* Booth in 1870 announced that he would convert the People's Market Whitechapel into a People's Mission Hall, featuring a shop, tea rooms, and a vast kitchen capable of serving 1,000 gallons of soup every day.

The Booths' open-air missions continued to attract violence by angry mobs, as well as troublemakers hired by pub owners, who feared the evangelists would take away their business. Police were inclined to blame the Booths for the provocations and dragged away the marchers, threatening to lock them up. Despite the opposition of the mobs and authorities alike, thousands not only converted but joined as volunteers in Booth's work.

Security improved once William and Catherine opened the People's Mission Hall. The poor came for food and warmth as well as protection from the mean streets, and stayed to hear the gospel preached. George Bernard Shaw, himself a poor young Irishman in London, pleaded that no one could preach God effectively to a man, woman, or child with an empty stomach. Like Dickens, Shaw held poverty itself to be society's sin. By contrast, the Booths accepted the wide breach between the rich and poor of their time, but agreed that poverty brought out the worst in people. So they fed both stomach and soul. Booth proclaimed:

We intend the People's Soup Kitchen to be a half-way house to the People's Mission Hall, and this satisfying of the outer man with bread that perishes, we hope will lead on to the satisfying of the inner man with the bread that comes from heaven.[8]

In public advertisements the Booths offered more: "Shelters for the homeless, food depots for the poor, and industrial workshops and homes for the workless."[9]

Although he was now firmly headquartered in East London, Booth's mission could not be confined to the slums of the capital. He already harbored international ambitions. By 1870, the *East London Evangelist* was renamed the *Christian Mission Magazine,* and the Booth organization became known simply as the Christian Mission.

Who would pay for all of this? Certainly not the poor to whom the Booths were devoted. As a family, they now lived securely on gifts, lodgers' rent, royalties, pamphlets, and lecture fees. But the organization's finances were another matter. Offerings at the Mission and other preaching stations covered barely one-third of its expenses. Although Catherine helped by preaching in affluent communities, William was obliged to run the soup plant as a commercial operation which would, over time, clear the Mission's debts. By 1872 he also enjoyed some income from five "Food for the Millions" shops—discount grocers to the poor. Eventually, the commercial ventures proved to be more of a distraction from the Mission than sources of revenue, and they were dropped.

PRACTICAL CHRISTIANITY

For all his evangelical focus on salvation for eternal life, Booth's Christianity was intensely practical. He regarded the poor as inhabitants of a world resembling Dante's vision of hell. The outer circle of this inferno included those who, though honest, were starving and homeless; the second by those trapped by their vices; and the third by those who lived by crime. Whether criminal or innocent, they had poverty in common, and their overwhelming recourse was drink. Gin was not only cheaper than food; but it also eased the pangs of hunger and deadened the spirit to misery and responsibility.

At this distance in time, and with the failure of Prohibition in the last century, it is difficult to appreciate how alcohol served as the handmaiden of misery and crime in the England of Booth, Dickens, and Shaw. But the temperance movement was not just moralistic and puritanical. Its leaders considered temperance to be utterly practical and necessary.

To illustrate: While still a bachelor in his twenties living in a boarding house, my wife's paternal grandfather was elected mayor of a poor mining town in Eastern Ohio. Alarmed that the workers were wasting their wages in the town's saloons, then abusing their wives and children, he closed the saloons on Sunday. His motive was not at all religious but simply humane. When a lynch mob of miners came to his boarding house waving a noose, the young mayor stared them down, and they dispersed to their homes. The saloons remained shut on the Sabbath.

In contemporary America we demand that our children "just say no" to drugs and alcohol, and we encourage sexual abstinence or at least safe sex among adolescents, because drugs and teen pregnancy produce and sustain an impoverished, crime-prone underclass. In his own time, Booth was hardly alone in believing that people could not be saved for God, society, and themselves unless they put down the bottle.

By 1881, Booth expanded his organization's ministry to include assistance to the thousands of prostitutes in the East End, offering them food, shelter, counsel, respectable work, and protection from their procurers. Soon the new ministry was extended to the victims of child abuse, especially very young girls who were virtually enslaved as servants in London's brothels.

In 1885 W. T. Stead, editor of *The Pall Mall Gazette,* published a series of four front-page articles exposing the trade in women and children. Booth himself arranged for a former brothel keeper, now a Salvationist, to stage a young girl's abduction to prove it could be done. Eliza Armstrong's mother sold her 13-year-old daughter, no questions asked, to Booth's surrogate, for 3 pounds. Eliza was taken to a brothel, where the editor of the *Gazette,* posing as a customer, put her at her ease. Then the girl was whisked off to Paris by another female Salvationist.

The exercise demonstrated that parents would sell a girl into prostitution and that the girl could be abducted to a foreign country.

The newspaper accounts were a sensation, with final copies of the paper selling for thirty times their cover price. Bernard Shaw so supported the expose that he volunteered to sell copies of the paper on street corners himself. Five years earlier, a thousand women had petitioned the prime minister to make changes in the law that would prohibit commerce in children. As a result of Booth's handling of the Eliza Armstrong case and his petition to Parliament signed by 393,000 citizens, the age of consent in Britain was raised to sixteen and brothels were outlawed.

THE ARMY

Although Booth served as general superintendent of the Mission, his disciples gradually abbreviated his title to "General." Over time, they began to characterize the mission in martial terms. The Yorkshire mission of 1877 in Whitby, for example, was advertised by posters that read:

WAR! WAR! IN WHITBY 2,000 MEN AND WOMEN
Wanted at once to join in the Hallelujah Army
That is making an attack on the devil's kingdom
every Sunday in ST. HILDA'S HALL.

By the following year, Booth's annual report proposed calling the Mission a "Volunteer Army." His son Branwell objected that he was not a volunteer but a "regular." On the spot his father crossed out the word "volunteer" and substituted "Salvation Army." Although he objected to his title of general as pretentious, it stuck. The Christian Mission magazine now became *The Salvationist*. Although members of the Booth family were slow to don uniforms themselves, the Salvationists were already identifying themselves by wearing red jerseys, kerchiefs, or arm bands. A red and blue flag with a bright yellow sun at its center preceded the Army in its marches.

Still the objects of persecution, the Salvationists now went on the offensive. Before a crowd of 4,000 in Tyneside Catherine declared:

The time has come for fire. All other agents have been tried: intellect, learning, fine buildings, wealth, respectability, numbers. The great men and the mighty men and the learned men have all tried to cast out these devils before you, and have failed. Try the fire! There are legions of the enemies of our great King. Fire on them. There are the legions of strong drink, damning millions; of uncleanness damning millions more; of debauchery, blasphemy, theft, millions more. Charge on them; pour the red-hot shot of the artillery of heaven on them, and they will fall by thousands.[10]

ASSAULT ON AMERICA

It was George Scott Railton, a Scotsman, who had suggested that the Mission be declared an Army. Railton was, if anything, even more of a promoter and showman than Booth himself and became the first of the older man's lieutenants. Still in his teens, Railton had journeyed alone to Morocco to convert the Muslims, or rather, to reconvert to Christianity those who pretended to be Muslims in order to get along. He carried a banner that proclaimed in English "Repentance—Faith—Holiness."

It was only with the aid of the British consul in Morocco that the young Scotsman escaped the wrath of the natives and was returned to England. On his return, he came across a booklet by Booth, *How to Reach the Masses with the Gospel*. At the age of twenty-four, Railton became a lifelong convert to the Mission. The Booth family took him into their home and hearts. It would be Railton who would lead the Salvation Army to the United States in 1880.

A year earlier, the monthly *Salvationist* was deemed inadequate to rally the troops and evangelize the poor, so Booth converted it into a weekly, producing 1,400 copies an hour, and shipping them in bulk on trains leaving London's many railway stations to blanket the rest of Britain.

The new publication, named *The War Cry,* sold for half a penny. "No more surrender; no more truce," proclaimed the inaugural edition.

As early as 1872, individual Salvationists had emigrated to the United States to organize Christian missions on Booth's pattern in Cleveland and later in Philadelphia. Booth was reluctant to recognize them officially. But in 1880, he tapped Railton to make an assault on America. The Scotsman, given the rank of Commissioner, chose 33-year-old Captain Emma Westbrook and six teenage "Hallelujah Lasses" as his soldiers.

As the party bid farewell to the Booths, Railton was in full uniform, consisting of navy blue trousers, red jersey, and coat with a high-fitting collar sporting a red badge with a yellow "S." The women likewise were in full Army uniform, with ankle-length navy dresses and thigh-length coats buttoned to the collar and trimmed with red. Their hats resembled English policemen's helmets, and were encircled with a red band proclaiming, in bright yellow type, "The Salvation Army."

"America for Jesus!" someone shouted at quayside, to which Railton answered "Amen!" On landing in New York after a perilous voyage, the party fell to their knees and claimed the former British colonies for Jesus. They were offered temporary use of a former brothel in Baxter Street for their meetings. Moreover, a vaudeville producer, Harry Hill, offered his theater on Sunday evening, believing the Salvationists would be entertaining.

Countering critics who argued that the Army would damage its reputation by appearing on a stage, Railton argued that, as yet, they had no reputation to lose. And so, just four days after arriving in America, posters appeared, reading:

SALVATION ARMY WILL ATTACK
KINGDOM OF THE DEVIL
HARRY HILL'S VARIETY THEATER
ON SUNDAY, MARCH 14, 1880
AT 6:30 P.M.
AFTER WHICH A PANORAMA OF UNCLE TOM'S CABIN
ADMISSION 25 CENTS

MISSION ON THE ICE

Railton managed to convert a notorious drunk the day of the performance. The news spread and the theater was packed for the evening debut of the Salvationists in the New World. But the crowd, expecting entertainment, was disappointed, and no one answered Railton's call for conversion. Moreover, New York's mayor forbade Railton and his troops from preaching or evangelizing in the city's streets, so Railton moved to Philadelphia. Within two months of arriving in America, he recruited nearly 500 soldiers, commissioned 16 officers, and opened a third mission in Newark.

By the following winter, he was in St. Louis and unable to rent a hall for meetings, because owners feared the large crowds would wreck their buildings. With a mad stroke of genius, he advertised that he would hold his meetings on the frozen Mississippi River, which required neither rent nor permit. Virtually destitute, Railton preached with his feet wrapped in newspaper and string, because he could not afford shoes. Although he spoke with fire on the ice, he made no converts that day. Remaining two months, he ate only rarely and slept on a pile of *War Crys.*

On New Year's Day 1881, Booth sent a cable calling his Commissioner home to England to administer what was already an international Army with missions in France, India, and Australia. He was replaced in America by Major Thomas E. More. More was a poor administrator who, when challenged by Booth, founded his own army, taking many Salvationists with him.

THE AMERICAN EXPERIENCE

Booth's first-ever trip abroad, in 1886, was intended to shore up the Army in the United States and Canada. The General was warmly received, not least by American Protestant clergymen, who welcomed him into their churches. In Britain, by contrast, he was the object of either the envy or indifference of the clergy. After a three-month tour, Booth returned permanently to London, leaving his son, Ballington, and Ballington's wife Maud as leaders of the North American command. Nine years later, Ballington defected to form the Volunteers of America. But eight years before his death, Booth made a better choice, appointing his daughter Evangeline as national commander. She would serve for thirty years.

Fast-forward to the millennium: Today the Salvation Army operates from 9,500 centers across the United States alone, serving thirty million needy Americans it refers to as "clients." Its work extends to every zip code in the nation; its annual budget exceeds $2 billion. The celebrated management consultant Peter Drucker has called the Army "the most effective organization in the United States. No one even comes close to it with respect to clarity of mission, ability to innovate, measurable results, dedication, and putting money to maximum use."[11]

Here is the organization's straightforward mission statement:

The Salvation Army, an international movement, is an evangelical part of the universal Christian Church. Its message is based on the Bible. Its ministry is motivated by the love of God. Its mission is to preach the gospel of Jesus Christ and to meet human needs in his name without discrimination.

Retired National Commander Robert A. Watson traces the basis of the Army's mission to two verses in Scripture: Jesus' command that his followers teach and baptize all nations (Matthew 28:19) and to their responsibility to serve the hungry, the thirsty, the naked, the homeless, the sick, and the persecuted (Matthew 25:40). "We don't consider the two aspects of our mission, to preach and to serve, as separate from one another," Watson explains. "We don't serve people who are hurting only to preach to them. And we don't preach without offering the example of service without discrimination. To us, the two obligations are inseparable."[12]

Predictably, public agencies that rely on the Salvation Army can be uncomfortable with the integrated mission, wanting only social services. Still, despite pressure to separate "church and state," the Army receives a quarter of a billion dollars annually from public and private agencies, including government at all levels. In the 1970s, the Army had a $100,000 contract with New York City to serve lunches to the poor in Harlem. After many years city officials balked at the Salvation Army's name remaining on the building where the lunches were served (it was the Army's own building), at saying grace over the meals, and at leading the elderly crowd in familiar hymns.

The Salvationists refused to back down, whereupon the contract was withdrawn by the city. When most of the hungry regulars refused to go anywhere else for a free lunch, the Army found a private source of funding for food and fellowship, and the service continued, along with hymns and grace.

REDEMPTION

In 1878, William Booth published the Army's creed, which borrowed from 1 Thessalonians 5:23:

We believe that it is the privilege of all believers to be 'wholly sanctified,' and that their 'whole spirit and soul and body' may be preserved blameless unto the coming of our Lord Jesus Christ.

The Army's work is not merely to clothe the naked, feed the hungry, and minister to the sick, but to redeem lives. Robert A. Watson calls "the real secret of our success" the ability to get people "to accept responsibility for integrating their hearts, their minds, their souls with transcendent purpose. We help them reconnect."[13]

Many charities in America function with staff whose salaries, expense accounts, and offices rival those of Fortune 500 corporations. The Salvation Army, by contrast, relies on a work force of 3.4 million that includes 3.3 million unpaid volunteers and 43,000 employees working out of storefronts and abandoned churches, plus 5,000 uniformed officers who, operating as couples, earn a pittance for their lives of total dedication.

Watson, the former National Commander, provides this job description:

We're looking for individuals and couples to undergo two years of intensive training at their own expense, wear a uniform their whole career, subsist on a fraction of what they might be paid elsewhere, and spend most of their time with the homeless, the drug addicted, and other desperate people. Successful candidates can expect to work long hours, often in inhospitable environments and, from time to time, in dangerous ones. The job combines the responsibilities of a country parson and a city social worker. Medical skills are always a plus. So is accounting. And it's important that applicants be able to: drive trucks, put on puppet shows, play the cornet, coach basketball, sing harmony, negotiate real estate deals, cook for hundreds, and solicit funds on city streets and corporate board rooms.

He asks, rhetorically: "Are the lines forming yet" to join up?[14]

And, of course, they are. How else explain the attraction of the Army's mission to 3.3 million volunteers? Not the uniforms, the brass bands, and the ubiquitous kettles and bells between Thanksgiving and Christmas, but the sheer effectiveness of turning hellish lives into something a bit more heavenly.

The Army operates by rules every bit as strict as those imposed by the Booths in their time. The Army's adult rehabilitation centers, for example, are not drop-in facilities but demand at least six months' residence and total sobriety, participation in individual and group counseling, skills training or formal education, and performance of house-keeping duties at the center.

Salvation Army officers are bound by even more stringent rules. Beyond persisting in faith and pursuing exemplary lives, they cannot marry anyone who does not also agree to become an officer. Officers move when ordered and accept the assignments given them. Moreover, they live in assigned housing. It is truly Army life.

Yet the movement is flexible. A small facility for unwed mothers in New York City grew over the years into a medical complex and teaching hospital involving nearly a thousand doctors. It bore Booth's name, but it was a budgetary burden to the Army, preventing it from putting resources to more pressing needs. So, swallowing their regrets, they sold the facility, reckoning that the overall mission was more important than a hospital honoring their founder.

Although the American Red Cross is more popularly associated with disaster relief, the Salvation Army rushes in to save and sustain lives. It is not unusual for the Army to commit a quarter of a million dollars in cash in a single day to a disaster zone without knowing where the money will come from. Within 20 minutes of the 1995 bombing of the Oklahoma City federal building, the Army had three canteens on site to serve rescue workers. When Hurricane Floyd wreaked havoc on the Atlantic coast in 1999, the Army assisted 18,000 people in the first twelve hours and remained for three months, contributing 200,000 hours to rebuilding homes and lives.

THE SUMMING-UP

In May, 1912, with but months to live, the 83-year-old William Booth, frail and nearly blind, addressed 10,000 Salvationists assembled in London's vast Albert Hall. It would prove to be his valedictory.

The old General reflected on what he might have been and what he actually was. "I might have chosen as my life's work the housing of the poor," he began, but reflected that hundreds of thousands of homeless had indeed been given shelter through his Army's efforts. "I might have given myself up to the material benefit of the working classes," he mused, but acknowledged "the tens of thousands who, but for the Army, might have been almost starved."

Booth pondered aloud whether he might better have concentrated the Army's energies on temperance reform or embraced a career as a physician. He answered by affirming that "tens of thousands of the most devilish and abandoned drunkards that the world has ever known have been reached and reclaimed," and noting that his Army had already founded twenty-four hospitals for the poor.

The old General wondered whether his Army might have made assistance to prisoners an earlier priority, and affirmed prison ministry as "a mighty work the Army is destined to do for the unhappy class" of criminals. As for choosing a political career, he added: "I might have tried to improve society by devoting myself to politics. But I saw something better than to belong to any Party—that by being the friend of every Party I was far more likely to secure the blessing of the multitude and the end I had in view."

Booth pronounced himself content with the direction of his life:

The object I chose all those years ago embraced every effort, contained in its heart the remedy for every form of misery and sin and wrong to be found upon the earth, and every method of reclamation needed by human nature. It is, of course, the Gospel of Jesus Christ.

Then he issued his troops a final challenge:

Is the Salvation War coming to an end? This war is just beginning. My part is coming to an end. But while I still have breath, I commit myself to strive for the Lord and those who need Him. While women weep, as they do now, I'll fight; while little children go hungry as they do now, I'll fight; while men go to prison, in and out, in and out, I'll fight; while there yet remains one dark soul without the light of God, I'll fight. I'll fight to the very end![15]

It was the General's last battle cry, and it was heard.

Chapter 9

The Catholic Worker Movement: The Virtue of Hospitality

We are not expecting utopia here on earth. But God meant things to be much easier than we have made them.[1]

Dorothy Day

The Catholic Worker movement is even less visible than the Salvation Army, but its clientele is much the same—the poor and addicted, the sick and hungry, the abused and abandoned, the homeless and unemployed.

To them they offer hospitality—in houses in the inner cities and on small farms in the American countryside. To create the best of all possible worlds for the neediest Americans, the Catholic Workers live in voluntary poverty themselves, begging for the provisions they share with the destitute.

Catholic Workers are not all Catholics or even Christians, but they are all volunteers, taking no salary and casting their lot with those they serve. Unlike most utopians, the Catholic Workers are community activists, picketing and striking and going to jail for just causes they believe would make for a fairer society. But their protest is nonviolent and their cause is "a green revolution—a radically new society where people will rely on the fruits of their toil and labor, cooperate freely for mutual assistance, and apply fairness to disputes."[2] They are an example to a disconnected society that we cannot receive unless we give.

Just as the Salvation Army was summoned to counter the sordid realities of life in Dickensian England, the Catholic Worker Movement was prompted by the human tragedies wrought by the Great Depression in the United States. But while the two initiatives continue to this day successfully confronting the physical and spiritual impoverishment of great masses of people, they differ in their spirit, expectations, and organization.

For starters, the Army is an organized charity, with a national headquarters, and a paid officer corps and civilian staff. By contrast, the Catholic Worker movement relies wholly on volunteers and boasts no headquarters, no officers, no salaries, and no board of directors. It consists wholly of autonomous "houses of hospitality," principally in the poorest sections of American cities, plus some working farms. Today there are more than 185 such communities. Few Catholic Worker houses are incorporated and some do not bother with local zoning regulations. They aim to be, in the pristine sense, counter-cultural, protesting the indifference and ameliorating the injustices of American society.

Whereas the Salvation Army contracts with government and private agencies to provide social services, boasting a $2 billion annual budget, the Catholic Worker movement rejects all ties to government. Its local leaders, all informally chosen, serve those in need by emulating their condition—embracing voluntary poverty themselves and begging for private contributions to continue their work. "Learn to beg," states its website's instructions for opening a new house, predicting that "you will receive all that you need." Its final instructions are "pray, pray, pray."[3]

Although Catholic Workers are not all Roman Catholics or even Christians, they have a distinctly non-Protestant approach to human nature and its redemption. Whereas evangelical Christians such as William and Catherine Booth sought to convert the poor to moral rectitude and a faith that guaranteed salvation, Catholic Workers make no demands on the faith or goodness of those they serve, and they offer no eternal promises. Rather, they serve with the sense that conversion and salvation are ongoing adventures, not decisions of a moment, so they are content to meet human needs without demanding faith or even gratitude. They focus not on eternal salvation, but on God's grace to manage each day.

MAY DAY

The movement was inaugurated on May Day, 1933 in Depression-bound New York City. It began with a tabloid newspaper, *The Catholic Worker,* that sold then (and still does) for a penny a copy. Some 2,500 copies were printed for the first issue.

That the movement was proclaimed in the midst of a huge Communist Party rally suggests its dual spirit of comradeship and contentiousness. While Catholic Workers reject collectivism as destructive of human dignity, they nevertheless believe that society must be improved in order that individuals be secure and fairly treated as their creator meant them to be.

To attract attention in Victorian England, the Salvation Army marched in the streets to hymns played by brass bands. By contrast, Catholic Workers are drawn to street demonstrations. Nonviolent protest is their badge of honor, and to spend a night in jail for one's convictions is considered not too great a price to pay to make a point about injustice. Their cofounder, Dorothy Day, acknowledged that Catholic Workers were not a disciplined army but "a large, untidy family," with all the eccentricities families have.

Nevertheless, they are drawn to organized protest. It is truly a *workers* movement, because its members consider the dignity of the individual to be exemplified in labor and productivity. When Cesar Chavez was organizing migrant farm workers in the 1960s to demand decent housing, wages, and job security, he came to the Christie Street Catholic Worker house in New York, which offered him and his staff housing and meals.

Tom Cornell, who has been with the movement for fifty-three years, recalls the collaboration:

I would take them to the offices of unions we worked with...the health workers union, the distributive workers, the butchers, and the taxicab drivers' unions to free up workers who would visit all the supermarket chains with us, their corporate headquarters, the stores themselves, and even the mom and pop (grocery stores). We had all the work done to set up the lettuce and grape boycott in New York, and it worked, the first successful boycott in America since the (Boston Tea Party).[4]

With their produce rotting on store shelves, the farmers backed down and recognized the union. The plight of the migrant workers improved because the supermarket chains were shamed into acknowledging the dire working conditions they had long ignored.

Cornell recalls that the nation's demonstrations against the Vietnam War dated from the day Catholic Workers in New York saw the celebrated newspaper photograph of a Buddhist monk immolating himself in Saigon. "We thought about it for a while and then...came up with an idea for what turned out to be the first demonstration against the war in Vietnam, just two of us, July 16, 1963. In ten days we had 250, in five years a million,"[5] he boasts.

THE ODD COUPLE

The Catholic Worker movement was founded by an American journalist, Dorothy Day, and an illegal immigrant, the French farmer-philosopher Peter Maurin. They had their Catholic faith in common, sharing a hunger for social justice, plus mutual admiration. Otherwise, they could hardly have been less alike in temperament and culture. Dorothy was a radical journalist and single mother, who had led a bohemian life and had spent time in jail. Her sympathies were with organized labor. Peter came from a poor family that had farmed the same fields in southern France for 1,500 years. Peter was theoretical, Dorothy practical, but both believed in the Sermon on the Mount and the social teachings of the modern popes. Together, from the depths of the Great Depression, they proposed to build a "new society within the shell of the old, a society in which it will be easier to be good."[6]

Despite their mutual affection, Dorothy and Peter remained celibate comrades all their days, married only to their movement to foster a cooperative and nonviolent social order free of extremes of wealth and poverty. Peter, the dreamer, proposed a new intellectual synthesis to meet humanity's material and spiritual needs. It would value prayer, culture, and labor. Through houses of hospitality in the cities and farming communes in the country, the poor and disenfranchised would be served, and they would be drawn into productive lives.

Unlike Dorothy, Peter was not a city person, but a man of the soil. He dreamed of city intellectuals being drawn into agriculture at the same time farmers became scholars in "cells of good living." In the city and on the farm, voluntary communities would meet regularly "for the clarification of thought," whereby people of all conditions and persuasions might explore the sicknesses of society and work for a cure.

Dorothy, born in New York City in 1897, was fully two decades Peter's junior. She grew up poor in New York, Oakland, and Chicago, and attended the University of Illinois, but did not graduate. Instead, barely out of her teens and shunned by her family, she took up radical journalism and worked for *The Liberator*. She was acting editor of *The Masses* when it was shut down by the U.S. Attorney General during the Red Scare following the Russian Revolution and World War I.

Jailed in 1917 for picketing the White House on behalf of women's suffrage, Dorothy at the age of twenty joined her fellow prisoners in a hunger strike. In Chicago she was jailed with prostitutes because of her ties to labor agitators. Before she joined with Peter Maurin, Dorothy moved easily in the society of socialists, anarchists, and communists, as well as fellow writers including Eugene O'Neill and Malcolm Cowley. A restless spirit, she moved to New Orleans to expose the harsh lives of taxi dancers by becoming one herself. She even took a turn at screenwriting in Hollywood, then lived in Mexico with the poor.

Falling in love with an atheist, she bore him a daughter out of wedlock. During the pregnancy, Dorothy became increasingly persuaded that God stood behind her aspirations for a better world. Wishing the best for her daughter, she had her baptized a Catholic, then followed her into the Church, whereupon the girl's father permanently separated from both of them.

THE MOVEMENT

The movement began in New York just five months after Dorothy and Peter were introduced. It was "Catholic" because they said it was, but it had no official standing within the Church and received no institutional assistance. Nor does it today. The couple sought neither authorization nor financing, just volunteers and private donations—a tradition that persists in the new millennium.

The Catholic Worker quickly reached a circulation of 150,000, only to plummet when patriotism trumped pacifism during the Spanish Civil War and World War II. The movement persisted in its nonviolent principles, and many volunteers and staff members were imprisoned or sent to public work camps in the 1940s for resisting the draft. Unlike Quakers and the Amish, Catholics could not appeal to their church's pacifist convictions.

Eventually the paper's circulation improved to nearly 100,000, and still appears seven times a year. A single copy typically has many readers and a long shelf life. During the Depression and war years, the houses of hospitality and farming communes multiplied. The movement expanded its mission to combat racism. As homelessness, addiction, teen pregnancy, and domestic violence increased, Catholic Workers added to their services to meet the needs of new victims.

Each Catholic Worker house or farm seeks to serve the peculiar needs of its locality. In Phoenix, for example, "Maggie's Place" is a home for pregnant women alone or in the streets. It also offers free art classes for children. "Andre House" in Berkeley, California, is a half-way house for men leaving prison. Berkeley's "Elizabeth House" is for women returning from jail to society.

"Magdalene House" in Half Moon Bay, California, offers housing to homeless families and migrant farm workers. In Oakland, another Catholic Worker community cares for Latin American refugees.

The "Temenos" Catholic Worker house in San Francisco proclaims itself the "presence of grace in the midst of despair, addiction, and violence of the street culture" in that city. Along with food, housing, and health care, it offers condoms and needle exchanges to reduce disease.

Across the country, in Hartford, Connecticut, "St. Martin de Porres House" operates a food coop and a summer youth camp for the poor. In Marietta, Georgia, the "Seamless Garment House" assists pregnant women, visits prisoners, and corresponds with inmates on Death Row. The list goes on: "Viva House" in Baltimore, serves 270 persons at every meal, and provides the poor with legal aid and children with after-school activities and summer camp. In Columbia, Missouri, Catholic Workers have organized to oppose assisted suicide, while the "Maurin-Day House" in Corpus Christi, Texas, provides the poor with a day shelter, where they can shower, do their laundry, and just sit and watch TV. In Houston, "Tomorrow's Bread Today" offers medical and home health care for the uninsured.

Some of the Catholic Worker communities have unique lifestyles. At the "Little Flower Catholic Worker Farm" in Goochland, Virginia, the diet is strictly vegetarian, and life is simple, with no television, computer, electricity, or plumbing. Its volunteers demonstrate for peace and serve meals to street people in the state capital. Meanwhile the "Alderson Hospitality House" in West Virginia, serves the families and friends of women in the nearby federal prison camp. Advertising for additional volunteers, the local Catholic Workers promise:

You'll sleep well in the cool mountain air, a must for anyone who loves a challenge and lives on the edge of the marginalized.

These are only a few examples of the more than 185 Catholic Worker communities across America. Despite differences in the local services they provide, they are all committed to nonviolence, voluntary poverty, prayer, and hospitality for the homeless, exiled, hungry, and forsaken. Together they continue to protest injustice, war, racism, and violence in all forms. They are peacemakers.

"TO OUR READERS"

The movement began with a tabloid newspaper, because it had not just services to offer, but the dream of a better world which it needed to explain. As Peter Maurin would argue, "The future will be different if we make the present different."

According to Dorothy, the first issue of *The Catholic Worker* was "planned, written, and edited in the kitchen of a tenement on 15th Street, on subway platforms, on the 'L,' and the ferry" in New York City. There was no editorial office, and no telephone, electricity, or salaries. "Next month someone may donate us an office. Who knows?"[7] Dorothy mused in her first editorial.

The cost of printing was partly covered by begging small donations from friends. The balance was squeezed out of the meager savings of the mendicant editors themselves, who postponed paying their personal utility bills to get the paper on the street. "By accepting delay," Dorothy wryly noted, "the utilities did not know that they were furthering the cause of social justice. They were, for the time being, unwitting cooperators" in the enterprise.[8]

Every new publication must target its readership even when it charges just a penny a copy. Dorothy dedicated *The Catholic Worker*:

- For those who are sitting on park benches in the warm spring sunlight.
- For those who are huddling in shelters trying to escape the rain.
- For those who are walking the streets in the all but futile search for work.
- For those who think that there is no hope for the future, no recognition of their plight—this little paper is addressed.
- It is printed to call their attention to the fact that the Catholic Church has a social program—to let them know that there are men of God who are working not only for their spiritual, but for their material welfare.[9]

Today, more than seventy years after the founding of the movement, one of every four Americans is a Roman Catholic. With the notable exception of poor Hispanic immigrants, the typical American Catholic in the twenty-first century is an educated white-collar, middle-class, conservative suburbanite, thoroughly assimilated into the prevailing culture. But at the time Dorothy and Peter began their movement, Catholics were more likely to be ethnic and blue-collar, without college credentials. Just as black Americans have traditionally looked to their own churches for support, the earlier generation of Catholics looked to theirs for affirmation.

ASSIMILATION VERSUS CHANGE

What they found was a church that sought to preserve its own identity at the same time it gained the respect of the nation's dominant Protestant culture. It was a church that commanded the devotion of its members but largely lacked a social agenda it could press on government. By contrast,

Dorothy and Peter believed that, for humanity's sake, the church must speak loudly to government and business alike.

"When religion has nothing to do with politics," Peter argued, "politics is only factionalism: 'Let's turn the rascals out so our good friends can get in.' When religion has nothing to do with business, business is only commercialism: 'Let's get what we can while the getting's good.'"[10]

At the same time it sought justice and jobs for workers, the movement decried government handouts while exalting personal responsibility. Peter recalled that the earliest Christians were admired by pagans for their personal generosity with one another: "See how they love one another." By contrast, Peter noted, the pagans of our time could only say, "See how they pass the buck" to others.

Dorothy and Peter wanted to transform an acquisitive society into a functional society—"from a society of go-getters to a society of go-givers."[11] Peter was fond of quoting his fellow-countryman Jean-Jacques Rousseau to the effect that when a person dies he can carry with him only what he has given away.

Although Peter complained that "strikes don't strike me," he joined with Dorothy in picketing and sitdown strikes. Dorothy could be almost cavalier about causes worthy of a public demonstration. "Again and again," she wrote, "we have helped workers on strike regardless of all talk as to whether the strike was just or unjust." Her motivation was two-fold: "It is never wrong to perform the Works of Mercy"; and because strikers "are enduring hardships and making sacrifices, they are in a receptive frame of mind."

She did not delude herself: "The workers are never going to be satisfied, no matter how much pay they get, no matter what their hours are." That is why "it is the social order which we wish to change," adding characteristically, that "the popes have hit the nail on the head. 'No man may outrage with impunity that human dignity which God Himself treats with reverence.'"[12]

Peter argued that generosity to the poor benefits everyone:

- To give to the poor is to enable the poor to buy.
- To enable the poor to buy is to improve the market.
- To improve the market is to improve business.
- To help business is to reduce unemployment.
- To reduce unemployment is to reduce crime.
- To reduce crime is to reduce taxation.
- So why not give to the poor
- For business' sake?

- For humanity's sake?
- For God's sake?

AMBASSADORS OF THE GODS

Peter was fond of quoting G.K. Chesterton to the effect that the Christian ideal has not been tried and found wanting, but has yet to be tried. He found it ironic that the ancient Greeks and contemporary Muslims were hospitable, while Christians could be callous. He told the needy:

Modern society calls the beggar bum and panhandler and gives him the bum's rush. But the Greeks used to say that people in need are the ambassadors of the gods....As God's ambassadors you should be given food, clothing, and shelter by those who are able to give it. Mahometan teachers tell us that God commands hospitality, and hospitality is still practiced in Mahometan countries. But the duty of hospitality is neither taught nor practiced in Christian countries.[13]

The creation of houses of hospitality did not originate with Dorothy and Peter. Rather, they revived a social institution, the settlement house, that had declined during the economic boom of the Roaring Twenties and nearly disappeared in the subsequent Depression. The best-known of such facilities was Hull House, established in Chicago in 1889 by Jane Addams, who patterned it after Toynbee Hall in London's destitute East End.

Hull House eventually encompassed thirteen buildings and a playground plus a children's summer camp in Wisconsin. For the most part its clients were poor immigrants and their families. Services included a day nursery, gymnasium, community kitchen, little theater, and a boarding club for working girls. College-level courses were offered in art, music, and crafts. Addams, who died at the age of sixty-four in 1935, pressed humanitarian causes that the Catholic Worker movement would promote from religious motives, among them racial and labor justice, universal suffrage, and children's rights. Like the Catholic Workers, Addams was a pacifist; she was awarded the Nobel Peace Prize in 1931.

Fast-forward to the spring of 2002, when *The Catholic Worker* published a platform aimed at making society more just and hospitable, and less acquisitive and material:

- In economics, it decried wide disparities in personal income, blaming those in power for living off the sweat of others' brows and robbing them of a just return for their work. It condemned as usury the charging of interest beyond administrative costs of loans and blamed it for the world debt crisis. It noted that homelessness and unemployment increase "in the midst of increasing affluence."

- In labor, it criticized the consumer society of disposable goods as trapping laborers "in work that does not contribute to human welfare." With the "unbridled extension of technology..." human need is no longer the reason for human work."

- In politics, it decried the priority placed by government on "military, scientific, and corporate interests" over those of individual human needs, and criticized bureaucracy as impersonal and insensitive.

- In morals, it noted rampant "spiritual destitution...manifested in isolation, madness, promiscuity, and violence," blaming it on "distorted images of the human person."

- In militarism, it identified "a direct connection between the arms race and destitution," and quoted the Second Vatican Council's finding that "the arms race is an utterly treacherous trap, and one which injures the poor to an intolerable degree."

A PLATFORM FOR PEACE

To cure a dysfunctional society, the movement advocates:

Personalism—"moving away from a self-centered individualism toward the good of the other" and "taking personal responsibility for changing conditions rather than looking to the state or other institutions to provide impersonal 'charity.'"

Decentralizing society—encouraging "family farms, rural and urban land trusts, worker ownership and management of small factories, homesteading projects, food, housing, and other cooperatives," with the aim of making money "merely a medium of exchange," and treating human beings as something more precious than mere "commodities."

A "green revolution"—"a radically new society where people will rely on the fruits of their own toil and labor," cooperate freely for mutual assistance, and apply fairness to disputes.

Nonviolence—"We oppose the deliberate taking of human life for any reason," preferring "to take suffering upon ourselves rather than inflict it on others." Proposed "means to establish peace" are "refusal to pay taxes for war, to register for conscription, (or) to comply with any unjust legislation." The platform promotes "participation in nonviolent strikes and boycotts, protests, and vigils," and withdrawal of support for dominant systems, corporate funding, or usurious practices."

Works of mercy—Encouraging personal generosity "so that the poor can receive what is, in justice, theirs, the second coat in our closet, the spare room in our home, a place at our table. Anything beyond what we immediately need belongs to those who go without."

Manual labor—The platform quotes Dorothy: "Besides inducing cooperation, besides overcoming barriers and establishing the spirit of sisterhood and brotherhood (besides just getting things done), manual labor enables us to use our bodies as well as our hands, or minds."

Voluntary poverty—Again she is quoted: "The mystery of poverty is that by sharing in it, making ourselves poor in giving to others, we increase our knowledge and belief in love."[14]

Dorothy was aware that many people looked upon pacifism as appeasement. Just after Pearl Harbor, a Catholic newspaper called her stand sentimental. She responded furiously in an editorial: "...let those who talk of softness, of sentimentality, come to live with us in cold, unheated houses in the slums. Let them come to live with the criminal, the unbalanced, the drunken, the degraded, the perverted. (It is not the decent poor, it is not the decent sinner who was the recipient of Christ's love)....Let their taste be mortified by the constant eating of insufficient food cooked in huge quantities for hundreds of people, the coarser foods, so that these will be enough to go around; and the smell of such cooking is often foul."

"Then," she concluded, "when they have lived with these comrades, with these sights and sounds, let our critics talk of sentimentality."[15] It was her conviction, against her church's doctrine of the just war, that no conflict in modern times could be just when civilians were the targeted victims of violence.

During the 1950s, Dorothy was jailed for protesting compulsory civil-defense drills against the nuclear threat. In the following decade, she went to Rome to press pacifism on the bishops at the Second Vatican Council. She obtained this concession: The Council agreed that modern nuclear war did not meet the church's just-war theory and was therefore immoral.

SAINT DOROTHY

In the interest of full disclosure, I should mention meeting Dorothy Day in the early 1950s when I was an undergraduate at Knox College. While working on this book, I was offered an opportunity to speak to the college community about the encounter:

I don't know how many students can claim to have encountered a saint in college, but I did here at Knox. In the 1950s it was still a time of compulsory chapel attendance, and I was asked to be student host for Dorothy Day, the founder of the Catholic Worker movement, who spoke to the college community about our common responsibility to care for the poor, the lonely, and the downtrodden. As I recall, we members of our so-called Silent Generation were pretty complacent and not much swayed either by Miss Day's appeal or by her example. But don't be surprised if one of these years she will be canonized as the next Saint Dorothy.[16]

Many people called Dorothy a saint during her lifetime. The flattery did not please her. "Don't call me a saint," she complained: "I don't want to be dismissed so easily." She explained: "When they call you a saint, it means basically that you are not to be taken seriously."[17]

Not everyone considered her saintly. Director J. Edgar Hoover wrote in her FBI file:

Dorothy Day is a very erratic and irresponsible person. She has engaged in activities which strongly suggest that she is consciously or unconsciously being used by communist groups. From past experience with her it is obvious she maintains a very hostile and belligerent attitude toward the Bureau and makes every effort to castigate the FBI whenever she feels so inclined.[18]

Hoover personally monitored Dorothy's activities throughout the war years and even before Pearl Harbor proposed "custodial detention in the event of a national emergency" for anyone like her who preached pacifism.

Dorothy shrugged off sanctity and delighted in self-deprecation. In later years, she enjoyed telling a story about visiting a couple whose young son, on meeting her, immediately burst into tears. The boy explained, "All day long they've been saying 'Dorothy Day is coming, Dorothy Day is coming.' And now you're here and you're just an old woman."[19]

Dorothy dismissed halos because she believed that everyone can do what saints do. "We are all called to be saints," she argued, acknowledging that "we might as well get over our bourgeois fear of the name. We might also get used to recognizing that there is some of the saint in all of us. Inasmuch as we are growing, putting off the old man and putting on Christ, there is some of the saint, the holy, the divine right there."[20]

Nevertheless, just three years after her death in 1980, a Catholic order initiated the labyrinthine process for having her officially canonized. Many of her colleagues objected, one of them declaring his "suspicion that the process is unworthy of the candidate." Biographer Robert Ellsberg noted on the centenary of her birth:

Many in the Catholic Worker expressed indifference or even hostility to the idea of canonizing Dorothy Day, feeling it would represent a cooptation of her witness. It would shift attention from imitation to veneration, a preoccupation with miracles, and so forth. It would cost money that could be spent on the poor. It would put too much emphasis on one person rather than the community she was part of. Inevitably, church officials would try to emphasize her "wonderful work" with the poor, her orthodox piety, her spirit of obedience and respect for the magisterium, and so would filter out the problematic areas of her life and witness—particularly her radical pacifism and her resistance to the state.[21]

A LONG LONELINESS

Toward the end of her life one of her biographers, Harvard psychiatrist Robert Coles, asked her how she would like to be remembered. After noting her pleasure in life's inevitable inconsistencies and contradictions,

She then took up the challenge and repeated...her wish to be defined and remembered as a member of a particular Christian community, as an ardent seeker after God who, with some devotion, had followed His example "after a few false starts." Then, after pausing to look out the window, after a retreat into silence, she said slowly "To be a witness does not consist in engaging in propaganda or even stirring people up, but in being a living mystery; it means to live in such a way that one's life would not make sense if God did not exist."[22]

In life's adversities Dorothy found solidarity with others. She acknowledged: "We have all known the long loneliness, and we have learned that the only solution is love, and that love comes with community."[23]

Dorothy was buried in a homespun dress and laid in a plain wooden casket, the gift of Trappist monks. In death, her only adornment was a icon hanging from a wood-beaded chain around her neck. On her casket rested a single flower and a ribbon bearing the inscription "Resurrection."

She was buried on Staten Island, where she had lived when she gave birth to her daughter. Her simple headstone bears the symbol of loaves and fishes, with which Jesus miraculously fed the multitudes. Her epitaph is equally simple: "Deo Gratias"—"Thanks be to God."

Chapter 10

Today's Utopias: A Place Just Right

And God saw everything that he had made, and behold, it was very good.[1]

Genesis

The quest to create the best of all possible worlds persists in America, but not simply in the thousands of intentional communities that seek to contrive a kind of heaven on earth for their members.

To be sure, every individual pursues happiness, but increasingly the quest is becoming a solitary pursuit, and the nation's social capital has suffered. For utopians happiness is a joint enterprise. It can only be achieved among people who share the harmony of common values and mutual caring.

Estimates of the number of utopian communities in the United States today run as high as 20,000, but there is no way of knowing the actual number. The Yellow Pages do not provide a listing in that category. Moreover, most contemporary communities shy from calling themselves utopian, favoring "intentional" instead, because they consider themselves to be not only idealistic but intensely practical.

The nearest thing to a trade association for utopians is the Fellowship for Intentional Community in Rutledge, Missouri. It shares information among its members and provides practical counsel on making communities work. In its directory, it carries comprehensive listings of some 600 communities in the United States and Canada plus 100 on other continents.[2] The Fellowship acknowledges that there are thousands of communities which are beyond its reach. Utopians are not necessarily joiners.

Compared to the grand movements of the past, contemporary communities are modest, compact, and inward-looking, favoring alternative life styles. Sociologist Rosabeth Moss Kanter notes that "overwhelmingly, the grand utopian visions of the past have been replaced by a concern for relations in a small group" with a focused agenda.[3]

Whereas utopian communities in the past considered themselves to be societies, their contemporary counterparts are inclined to refer themselves as families. Many communes are legacies of the counter-culture of the 1960s. Rather than attempting to transform the larger society, many utopians have given up on it, leaving to pursue their own modest values with like-minded compatriots. Like Voltaire's disillusioned hero, Candide, they concentrate their energies on making their own gardens grow.

As their scope and size have diminished, however, their variety has increased. A significant number of intentional communities, far from pursuing their own communal self-interest, serve the needs of the poor, the homeless, sick, and addicted, the immigrant and the prisoner. Still, they lack the size, impact, vision, and ambition of movements like the Salvation Army and Catholic Worker.

PROFILES OF PARADISE

Twenty-first-century American utopian communities are characterized by remarkable similarities as well as distinct differences. Most included in the Fellowship are modest in size, some with just two members. Few boast more than 100, but some, like Adidam in California, have over 1,000. The Hutterites number 40,000 members in 389 colonies, principally in the American and Canadian West.

California is home to the largest number of intentional communities, followed by Michigan and Washington state. Most communities are rural, but there are multiple communities in New York City, Philadelphia, Chicago, and other large cities. Few extant communities were formed before the 1960s, but the Collegiate Living Organization in Florida dates from 1931 and Michigan's Osterweil Cooperative from 1946.

There are distinct types of intentional communities. One-fourth describe themselves as cooperative houses, 17 percent as ecovillages, 16 percent as cohousing, 13 percent as intentional neighborhoods, 11 percent as communes, 10 percent as land trusts or coops, and only 8 percent as strictly religious communities. But most consider themselves to be spiritually motivated. The vast majority of communities govern themselves by consensus or majority rule. Nearly all welcome new adult members. Of those communities with children, most are open to more youngsters, and a few provide home schooling by community members.

Most communities are open to both men and women in roughly equal numbers. There is more diversity in ownership of communal property. Most communes indicate ownership by committee, some by land trusts, a few by individuals and even landlords. Some communities apply for nonprofit status; others operate a variety of small businesses. Most seek to be sustainable economically, but not profitable.

In the effort to be self-sustaining, rural communes with some acreage attempt to grow as much as half the food they consume, and most favor some organic food in their diet. A substantial minority of communities are either vegetarian or proscribe red meat. The members of nearly all communities join for at least one common meal every day. Most permit alcohol in moderation; fewer tolerate the use of tobacco. None acknowledge the use of drugs.

A substantial minority of intentional communities openly welcome gay and lesbian members. But many, if not most, gay communitarians prefer to join integrated communities in which heterosexuals are the majority because they relish the diversity. Still, there are more than seventy-five known communities set aside for lesbian membership alone, and yet others restricted to gay men.

OF CULTS AND COMMUNES

The great utopian movements of the past were overwhelmingly motivated by religious faith and the need to serve society. By contrast, the majority of utopians today espouse ideals that are simply secular and self-serving. Nevertheless, many insist their members follow a "spiritual path." Here is how a fairly representative handful of communities briefly describe themselves:

- Loving and sustainable culture
- Hands-on spirit/earth connection
- Prayer, poverty, nonviolence
- Community, ecology, and health
- Doing the works of mercy
- Learn/grow good food and friends
- God, community, transformation
- Social responsibility
- Permaculture and alternative technology.

Contemporary communities ask not to be confused with religious cults. Unlike cults, they do not practice brain-washing. With exceptions, they are not led by charismatic dictators or gurus. Community discipline is typically established by consensus, not blind obedience. Members are free to communicate with their families and the outside world, and to leave at any time.

Most groups favor common ownership of property but, unlike cults, do not confiscate their members' savings. Although some intentional communities are critical of the larger society, they do not consider the outside world to be evil or a threat. Nor are they bound by a millennial vision of a future Armageddon in which they will prevail while the world perishes. Nevertheless, most utopians separate themselves from the larger society to seek a better life.

Twin Oaks is in many ways representative of utopian communities dating from the 1960s that have not only survived but also have flourished in the new millennium. It describes itself as "an ecovillage of 100 people living on 450 acres of farmland and forestland in rural Virginia." Its life-style is motivated less by religious faith than by "values of egalitarianism, ecology, and nonviolence." As a salute to earlier utopias, it calls one of its buildings "Oneida."

The community is economically self-sufficient, due to income it produces and income shared by members who have outside jobs. Making hammocks, chairs, and tofu, plus indexing books occupies about a third of its members' labor, leaving the remainder for "a variety of tasks that benefit our quality of life," including organic gardening, milking cows, and constructing and maintaining their own buildings.

Over the decades, Twin Oaks has developed an elaborate community culture that includes "social and support groups, performances, music, games, dance, and art." It is a do-it-yourself culture: "We share our vehicles, we build our own buildings, and we have little internal use of money." Outside the community its members work actively for "peace and justice, ecology, and feminism."[4]

ROMANTIC RHETORIC AND GROWING PAINS

John Leonard spoke for contemporary utopians when he acknowledged in 1971:

The romantic notion of the perfectibility of man is really all we have to sustain us, no matter how illusory it may prove to be...The rest is rhetoric, and the romantics have the best rhetoric.[5]

Twin Oaks cherishes a romantic link with utopian communities of America's past. Not only is its community house named for Oneida, but the commune's workshop is called Harmony, after Robert Owen's nineteenth-century village of New Harmony in Indiana. The original farmhouse on the site, now the kitchen and refectory, is named Llano for an early twentieth-century socialist community.

The commune's immediate inspiration came from a 1948 novel, *Walden Two*, by a celebrated Harvard psychologist. B.F. Skinner, a founder of behaviorism, proposed that communities would function better and people would be happier if good behavior was reinforced by rewards. Twin Oaks was founded by eight people who met at a Walden Two conference in Ann Arbor, Michigan in 1966. The following year, one of the eight supplied the money to purchase 123 acres near Richmond, including fields formerly used to grow tobacco. Within four years, Twin Oaks was home to thirty-six members and ten visitors, but only two of the original eight founders remained.

Farming and hammock making were inadequate to support a community of that size, so eight members took outside jobs on a rotating basis to bring in $50 or more each week. The group flirted briefly with the dream of operating a country store, but the idea never materialized.

Yale University sociologist Rosabeth Moss Kanter visited Twin Oaks in its early years and found its organization superior to the many casual (and short lived) communes then proliferating.

She noted that is was organized and growing, that it had clear and strict rules, and that it found no fault with technology or commerce. Members tended to be white, from middle-class families, and still in their twenties, but even in the early years, the community attracted some professionals already in their forties.

The community was health conscious from the outset. Unlike other communes of the sixties and seventies, it was drug-free, and it provided its members annual medical examinations from its own assets. Twin Oaks society is orderly and serious minded, even earnest. Professor Kanter noted:

Signs are everywhere: a sign on a tattered towel in the laundry room points out what happens when bleach is undiluted; a bent record demonstrates the consequences of leaving records on top of the heater. There is a place for everything and everything is in its place.[6]

A SOCIETY WITHOUT HEROES

What distinguishes a successful intentional community from a family summer camp is its values. From its founding, Twin Oaks was driven by the quest for equality and social justice. Accordingly, it makes no distinctions of sex, race, education, intelligence, or age. But it goes much further than any Equal Opportunity employer:

We will not use titles of any kind among us. All members are "equal" in the sense that all are entitled to the same privileges, advantages, and respect. This is the reason we shun honorifics of any kind, including "Mrs.," "Dr.," "Mother," "Dad," etc....All members are required to explain their work to any other member who desires to learn it....Observing this rule makes it impossible for any member to exert pressure on the community by having a monopoly on any certain skill....Seniority is never discussed among us. This is because we wish to avoid the emergence of prestige groups of any kind....We will not boast of individual accomplishments. We are trying to create a society without heroes. We are all expected to do our best....[7]

At Twin Oaks, members discard their family names. Some have changed both their names and careers to separate themselves from their previous lives. Employment in the commune is gender-neutral: men are as likely to work in the kitchen and women in the shop and fields. With the exception of small personal items, all property is held and owned in common, including earnings from any member's employment outside the community. All services and goods, including clothing, are provided by the community, along with a tiny weekly cash allowance for individual needs. Even clothing is shared.

Still, individuality is honored, and privacy is respected in the community. Members' rooms may not be entered without permission. When goods or services must be purchased, the community as a whole establishes priorities. Early in its history one member required an expensive operation and hospitalization. Other members sold their blood at $15 a pint to help pay the costs.

At Twin Oaks equality and responsibility go hand in hand. Like Oneida in the nineteenth century, the contemporary commune is meticulously managed. In its early years, there were more tasks to be managed at Twin Oaks than members to handle them, so several members took on multiple tasks, including budgeting and fulfillment. But its managers are not bosses. I am reminded of my own experience as a graduate student in Paris in the 1960s when I managed a social center for foreign students near the Sorbonne. Since the center was self-governing, my title in French was simply *Responsable*. I possessed no authority, just responsibility for things going smoothly.

LABOR AND DECISION-MAKING

It is not surprising that most intentional communities fail before their fifth birthday. Like small businesses, they begin typically full of hope but short on funding. There are additional handicaps. One is how to distribute the workload. Some tasks are more onerous and unattractive than others. The Oneida Community in the nineteenth century became prosperous enough that it was able to hire outsider laborers for the hard and unpleasant tasks. But in the typical commune, its members must handle all the tasks themselves.

Twin Oaks attempts to solve the problem of work equity by issuing labor credits. Each member is required to earn the same number of credits every week. The credits are calculated by the number of hours worked multiplied by a factor from .9 to 1.5. The easier or more enjoyable jobs are assigned the lowest factors; the harder or odious tasks have higher factors. Theoretically, one could enjoy a short work week by choosing only those jobs no one else wanted. Early on, when the commune's septic tank needed cleaning, the low bidder for the nasty job agreed to two credits per hour. To keep her company, other members read poetry to her, earning only a fraction of her job credits for their efforts.

Rosabeth Moss Kanter notes that "the effectiveness of Twin Oaks' work system depends on the members' willingness to abide by it. Members set their own pace and often their own hours, and record their time worked." But she records several attempts to "beat the system":

One member indicated that people can fill out preference lists so that they must be assigned low preference tasks, receive more credit for them, and therefore work fewer hours. He complained that there was no effective way to counteract this situation, except by criticizing such people to their face since it is considered inappropriate to gossip; yet these same people were the ones least likely to attend the weekly, voluntary feedback meetings. . .In its early days Twin Oaks included a poet who insisted that his art was more important than were communal chores, but he, like everyone, was expected to earn his assigned credits every week. A friend intervened by filling out his work sheet for him so that they would both be assigned to the same job, like dishwashing, and then she did the work for both of them.[8]

The ruse was discovered, the poet was asked to leave the community, and his friend soon joined him.

Another problem unique to communities of equals is how to make decisions. Simple democracy is usually inadequate because it means counting votes for and against a proposal. Some members will be winners, some losers. When I managed the church-sponsored student center in Paris, I was assisted by a group of volunteers, most of them French. In one meeting, having failed to reach consensus, I made the mistake of calling for a vote. One of the volunteers pulled me aside. "Votes are no good," he advised. "Those who lose will leave the center altogether."

Unlike the French, with their proliferation of political factions, Americans are accustomed to just two major parties. But in utopia, every individual can be a party unto himself or herself. How can one escape utter anarchy?

CONFLICT AND CONSENSUS

In a profit-making business, there is a product or service, and people are paid for their work contributions. During my own working years, notably in journalism, I most enjoyed being responsible for supplying a product and meeting a payroll. When I was a supervisor, everyone knew it. When I worked for someone else, I knew who it was. I could ask for a raise. I could be fired for being nonproductive or obnoxious.

Working in a *nonprofit* setting is something else altogether. There is still a product or service, of course, but work is motivated by idealism, not gain. Staff tend to work for less pay than in commercial business, and there is reliance on volunteers. Decisions tend to be made by committees; even supervisors are subject to them. Staff are inclined to think that their labor involves personal sacrifice; volunteers must be thanked and occasionally coddled. Supervisors must satisfy many constituencies.

A utopian community has all of the drawbacks of a nonprofit and none of the advantages of the profit-making enterprise. Strictly speaking, there is no product. The members "serve" one another to create a satisfying lifestyle. Beyond that, there is no economic incentive, because utopias typically seek no more than subsistence. There is no hiring or firing. Managers must satisfy the members, not the other way around. Even rules must be forged by consensus.

Originally, Twin Oaks' eight founders attempted to run the community by anarchy. The experiment failed because no one accepted ultimate responsibility. Subsequently, the community developed a system of rotating leadership by three "planners," each of whom served eighteen months, the terms staggered at six-month intervals. The troika was self-perpetuating, but any candidate could be vetoed by a majority of the membership by private balloting. In the beginning, the planners had so much responsibility and so little real authority that few chose to complete their full terms.

Consensus usually means that everyone does not necessarily prefer a given plan of action, but agrees that something must be done, and yields to the course that most in the group favor. The alternative is to do nothing. My wife and I are members of a Quaker meeting whose tradition holds that even consensus is inadequate as a decision-making device; only unanimity is acceptable. Predictably, a Quaker business meeting would try the patience of Job. There is no debate, but rather protracted silences as the members wait for divine guidance before speaking. As a consequence, much is postponed or left undone. A pre–Civil War carriage house adjacent to the meeting house collapsed when it was struck by a tree during a storm. Should it be rebuilt or torn down? As yet, there is no "sense of the meeting" signaling a unanimous decision, so the carriage house roof is propped up by timbers, an eyesore and a hazard. When Sunday School teachers brought a legitimate complaint that there was inadequate classroom space for a growing number of children, everyone acknowledged the problem, but there was no agreement about what to do except to muddle through, which is what the community is doing.

LIVING THE SERMON ON THE MOUNT

Although some contemporary utopian communities are motivated by secular humanism, religious faith continues to drive the quest to create heaven on earth.

The Bruderhof, a society that lives simply with the Sermon on the Mount as its sole rule, has seven active communities in the United States, two in England, and one in Australia. It was born in Germany in the aftermath of the World War I but is long since thoroughly Americanized. One of the movement's early members recalls:

It all began with discussions in Berlin. Often as many as 80 or 100 people came—workers, artists, students, atheists, evangelicals, anarchists, Quakers. Our discussions centered around the Sermon on the Mount, and the question burning in all of us was, "What shall we do?" Everyone knew their lives had to be changed. But there had to be action. We were tired of words.[9]

Maverick German theologian Eberhard Arnold decided that what must be done was to create communities that exemplified Jesus' teaching. He envisioned his Bruderhof ("Place of Brothers") as emulating the primitive Christian community described in the Acts of the Apostles, renouncing private property and living in prayer, fellowship, nonviolence, and respect for life.

The original communities Arnold founded in Germany resisted the rise of Nazism for four years. Expelled by Hitler in 1937, they re-formed in England in the late 1930s, then in Paraguay in the 1940s. At the end of World War II, brothers and sisters came to the United States to raise funds for a private hospital the Bruderhof operated in South America. Here they encountered young Americans who had been conscientious objectors during the war and yearned for a peaceful life in community. In 1954, the first American Bruderhof community, Woodcrest, was founded in Rifton, NY, two hours north of New York City.

Like many rural communes, the Bruderhof began with farming but soon found that additional sources of income were needed to support their communities. Today they manufacture and market children's furniture and toys as well as specialized equipment for people with physical disabilities. They are fond of quoting Kahlil Gibran that "work is love made visible," adding that "to us, the person who mops the floor is no less important than the one who practices medicine: we see our work as the practical way to express our love for each other, and as such, everything we do is much more than just a 'job.'"

Although some of the 2,000 members are unmarried, each community is based on the family. The Bruderhof provide nursery school and education through junior high school within the community, along with medical and dental care.

A LIFETIME COMMITMENT

With the Amish and Mennonites, the Bruderhof share an Anabaptist legacy. Superficially it is exemplified in plain dress, simple living, and the primacy of work and prayer. More substantively, it is reflected in their vows, which include lifetime commitment to the community. Parents encourage their children to explore opportunities outside the community before considering that adult commitment. Even when avowed members abandon the community, they may still return because "in the end, our commitment depends not on human willpower but on the grace of God."

Bruderhof communities do not proselytize, but they welcome visitors and new members. Although they pay taxes, they oppose the use of violence, even in the national defense. They envision a society that, in the words of Quaker founder George Fox, "takes away the occasion for war." A peace-loving people, the Bruderhof are activists in the sense that they believe the Gospel has clear social implications. Accordingly, they align themselves "with the poor, the downtrodden, and the disenfranchised," but refuse to avenge their exploitation.

Their modest numbers have not prevented the Bruderhof from gaining the attention of many nonutopians through their Plough Publishing House, which not only prints its own titles but also sells other publishers' books by catalog. Plough's purpose is "to challenge the assumptions of institutional Christendom, to encourage self-examination, discussion, and nonviolent action, to share hope, and to build community." For a sect with Anabaptist roots, the Bruderhof are remarkably ecumenical.

As radical Christians, they believe that Jesus has the answer, or is the answer, to all of life's questions—economic, social, educational, political, and even personal—and that only in community can people discover those answers. Much as they prize community, they are wary of institutional religion. "Christian community," they argue, "can never be a lifestyle or an institution. It must remain a free-flowing movement that is driven by—and that will die without—the wind of the Holy Spirit."

To preclude differences within the community, the Bruderhof have a strict rule against gossip. According to Eberhard Arnold,

There must never be talk, either in open remarks or by insinuation, against any brother or sister, or against their individual characteristics—and under no circumstances behind their back. Gossiping in one's family is no exception. Without this rule of silence there can be no loyalty and thus no community.

Members are charged with confronting one another directly with complaints. If that fails, they must "draw in a third person whom both of them trust. In this way they can be led to a solution that unites them on the highest and deepest levels."[10]

THE HUTTERITES

With 40,000 members, the Hutterites constitute the largest egalitarian utopian community in America. Arguably, they are strong because their communities are based on religious faith. The twenty-eight members of "Forty Mile," a Hutterite community in Montana, find happiness in simplicity, hard work, and comradeship. Their outpost is so-named because it is 40 miles from the nearest town, although convenient Interstate 90 cuts through its 50,000 acres. Forty Mile is an offshoot of another colony that got too large (120 members seems to the faithful to be the maximum number for a workable utopia).

The Hutterites, members of a sect that began in sixteenth-century Moravia, live a modified form of Christian primitivism, holding property in common. Their homes are spartan. Their church at "Forty Mile" is a battered trailer. Like workable communities of the past, the families seek only "sustainability," sensing that easy living makes for bad Christians. Yet they eat well, enjoy their companions, and are grateful to their creator.

They struggle but are successful. Montana's 39 Hutterite colonies produce 60 percent of the state's pork, half its eggs, and 17 percent of its milk. Although they are, like many utopians, a people apart, they get along well with their neighbors, never locking their doors or closing their gates.

IN SEARCH OF THE PERFECT VILLAGE

Mohamed Atta, the lead terrorist in the September 11 attacks on the World Trade Center and the Pentagon, was persuaded that by his suicide he would merit the eternal reward of a paradise of pleasure where he would be served by beautiful women.

Practical utopians profess a more modest definition of the good life, holding that individual satisfaction is derived not from self-indulgence but from the close company of others possessed of like minds and hearts.

Short of abandoning one's possessions to embrace the common life, there are approximations of utopian living available to many Americans. For my wife and me, it would consist of living in a village. Becky was raised in a small Ohio town, going through elementary and high school with the same cohort of friends. Every summer, these many years later, they arrange a reunion.

I was raised in Chicago but was blessed to pass my teens in a small suburban village where I worked behind the soda fountain in its one family-owned drug store. Despite its small scale, village life was complete. We knew our neighbors. We did not feel compelled to lock our doors or our cars. When Becky and I each attended small liberal arts colleges, we found new friends, and the same easy intimacy prevailed. To this day, our closest friends are the ones we made long ago in those little communities.

For the past dozen summers, Becky and I have indulged our love of village life by exchanging homes with English and Scottish couples who live in communities as modest and charming as Brigadoon. Although I laugh as much as anyone at the foibles of the residents of Garrison Keilor's fictional Lake Wobegon, I could live contentedly in such a place were it not for the harsh Minnesota winters.

The Walt Disney Company has removed my objection by locating its version of a utopian village in Florida near Orlando. On 49,000 acres of lush land, it has created a town Norman Rockwell would find congenial. Celebration, Florida is peaceful and picturesque, full of houses with porch swings and picket fences. Kids play in the streets. Grown-ups chat with their neighbors. Churches abound. You can imagine Andy Hardy or even Tom Sawyer living down the street in this new-old village, which is expected to grow into a town of 20,000 as early as 2010.

A PLACE JUST RIGHT

To create Celebration, Disney in the late 1980s gathered well-known architects, studied attractive places such as Charleston, Savannah, and Coral Gables, and assembled focus groups of families who hankered for a taste of utopian living. Disney discovered that people wanted all the modern conveniences, but hidden in traditional home styles. So Celebration has front porches, back alleyways, colonial townhouses, and classical cottages, but fiber-optic wiring as well.

To foster a sense of community, there is an old-fashioned lakeside town center, complete with town hall, post office, library, deli, restaurants, bookstore-cafe, grocery store, dry cleaner, and a 500-seat cinema. Rather than building a simple hospital, there is a complete Health Campus.

The public school adjacent to the town center is operated by Osceola County, but Disney has invested heavily in its facilities, including an academy for lifelong learning. There are tennis courts, a golf course, and trails for hiking and biking. In Celebration, automobiles are accommodated but not allowed to put a distance between neighbors. Like all planned communities, Celebration has a long list of covenants promoting community while discouraging individual eccentricity.

Charles Fraser, one of Disney's consultants, believes that computer simulation will accelerate the creation of many more villages and towns across America on the Celebration model, and that large pension funds will invest in their development. There are likely to be nearly eighty million more Americans by 2025. "We need 3,000–4,000 Celebrations just to scratch the surface of their needs,"[11] Fraser predicts.

Of course, not everyone can afford to live in villages like Celebration. A simple, satisfying life does not necessarily come cheap. But utopians argue that enjoying the good life is just a matter of establishing priorities. Do we find our satisfaction in things or in other people? If our answer is "other people," we may have the makings of utopians.

Americans cannot have it both ways in any case. Strictly speaking, the quest for *self*-satisfaction is fraudulent. A solitary, autonomous, self-sufficient life, however rich, cannot compete with intimacy and connectedness with others. As God himself mused at the creation, "It is not good for man to be alone." That may be reason enough to join in the effort to create heaven on earth.

Author's Notes and Acknowledgments

This is my third attempt at accounting for the continuing quest for heaven on earth. My first effort failed because I had spread my net too widely, seeking to include utopian visions from literature. With a second effort, I focused on actual movements to embrace community in America. But it included efforts that were motivated by secular as well as spiritual aspirations.

With this third draft, I have largely confined myself to successful utopian movements in America motivated by religious faith. Any attempt to create heaven on earth is more likely to succeed if one happens to believe there is a real heaven to emulate—or a biblical paradise to restore.

Most of my books have suggested their sequels. In *Ten Thoughts to Take Into Eternity,* I surveyed the landscape of the afterlife and became curious about human attempts to approximate heaven this side of eternity. In *The Future of Christian Faith in America,* I identified the American Dream as utopian and determined to learn more about our national obsession with the good life for all. In *What Are We to Do?* I sketched a brief profile of Dorothy Day and became anxious to share more about that great woman's vision of the Sermon on the Mount as a blueprint for the best of all possible worlds. An early essay on the colonial Quakers was included in *How the Quakers Invented America.*

This is my most ambitious book to date. I credit my sources in the text and bibliography, but I want to express particular gratitude to Rosabeth

Moss Kanter for her book, *Commitment and Community.* Although it is now somewhat dated, it offers the best analysis by far of what it takes to be a practical utopian in America. Robert D. Putnam, in his *Bowling Alone,* has not only brilliantly explored the extent of our nation's secular and spiritual disconnectedness, but has suggested how we might go about restoring community. The book you hold is about people who believe the essence of heaven is life in community and that it can be approximated here on earth.

America's Spiritual Utopias is dedicated to Max L. Carter, campus minister and director of Friends Center at North Carolina's Guilford College. Since Max teaches a course on utopian communities, I asked him to recommend sources. Lecturing at Guilford in late 2001, I fell under Max's Quaker spell of friendly persuasion.

I am grateful for the encouragement of my editors, Suzanne Staszak-Silva, and Manohari Thayuman as well as Quaker Friends and fellow trustees of the Washington Theological Consortium. Sam Hine of The Bruderhof kindly helped me understand that exemplary utopian community. Retired Trappist abbot Mark Delery of Holy Cross Abbey and Benedictine Father James A. Wisemen of St. Anselm's Abbey helped me locate sources for my chapter on the cloistered life. Above all, I thank my wife, Rebecca, for the many improvements she suggested in the text. *America's Spiritual Utopias* is better because of *my* better half. Since I met Becky I have lived in the best of all possible worlds.

If you have comments about this book, I invite you to share them with me c/o P.O. Box 2758, Woodbridge, VA 22195 or *dyount@erols.com.* You can read my weekly syndicated column, "Amazing Grace," at *www.scripps news.com* by keying-in my name.

Timeline: Intentional Communities through the Ages

Sixth Century BCE	Buddha's followers rejected wealth, turned to meditation, and joined together in ashrams to model an orderly, productive, and spiritual way to live.
Second Century BCE	Essene communities flourished, based on Old Testament law. Their *Dead Sea Scrolls* likely provided a matrix for early Christian monastics.
First Century CE	Early Christians banded together in "communities of goods" (described in Acts 2:44–45).
Fourth Century CE	The first Christian monastic communities were established, with vows of poverty, chastity, and obedience, and a life of religious seclusion from the world.
1527	Hutterian Brethren were founded—Anabaptists practicing common ownership.
1540s	Mennonites, a sect of radical Anabaptists, began living in community, using the Bible as the only rule.
1620	Puritans founded Plymouth Colony based on simplicity.
1649	The Diggers—common folks who revolted against the British nobility—communally occupied Crown lands.

1698   The Amish (founded by Jacob Ammon) created communities, and insisted on strict interpretation of the Mennonite principles.

1774   The Shakers (founded by Mother Ann Lee) pursued spirituality, dancing, singing, celibacy, inventions, and handcrafts.

1825   New Harmony was founded by Robert Owen as a nonreligious experimental "village of unity and cooperation."

1825   Nashoba was founded by Francis Wright, to train Negroes for freedom" and help them earn their own sale price.

1841   Brook Farm was started, "an experiment in humane living to be achieved through education and discussion." It drew intellectuals such as Ralph Waldo Emerson and Nathaniel Hawthorne.

1848   Oneida Community was founded by John Humphrey Noyes, based on the practice of "complex marriage."

1855   The Amana Colonies were established in Iowa by German Protestants seeking Christian community.

1889   Hull House was founded in Chicago by Jane Addams, to "create a human community offering protection against the anonymous city."

1900   Arden was founded in Delaware, based on the Single Tax Theory proposed by economist Henry George.

1910   Degania was founded in Israel, the first of 269 kibbutzim (Jewish communal societies), with a mixed agricultural and industrial economic base.

1913   Gould Farm was founded to provide a community environment for the psychiatric treatment and rehabilitation of emotionally exhausted and disturbed people.

1920   Darvell, the first community of the Bruderhof network, was founded, based on a life of Christian brotherhood.

1924   Krotona Institute was established as a center of Theosophy, a philosophy that brings together science and religion, East and West.

1933   The Catholic Worker movement was founded by Dorothy Day and Peter Maurin, to raise socioeconomic consciousness through political agitation, nonviolent resistance, and voluntary poverty.

1937   The first coop house was started in what became the Inter-Cooperative Council (ICC), a network of nineteen student housing coops in Ann Arbor, Michigan.

1939   Several greenbelt "new towns" were created, as part of the U.S. Government's "New Deal" program.

1942   Koinonia was founded in Georgia by preacher Clarence Jordan, to promote racial reconciliation, in response to violence by whites toward blacks.

1946   Sunrise Ranch was established, the first community in the international "Emissaries" network.

1948   The FIC (originally named the "Fellowship of Intentional Communities") was established to provide connections and support among existing communities.

1955   The Ananda Marga network was founded by Shrii Anandamurti, to bring about a universal society based on love and Cosmic Brotherhood.

1956   Mitraniketan was founded—a nonpolitical, nonsectarian rural educational community that encouraged people to "think globally and act locally" and to develop the whole individual.

1957   Reba Place Fellowship was founded—an ecumenical lay community with a common purse.

1958   Yamagishism Life, large-scale agricultural cooperative communities, were founded in Japan.

1962   Findhorn was established in rural Scotland, as a "center of light" in harmony with nature's intelligence.

1964   L'Arche communities were founded by Jean Vernier, for developmentally disabled and those wanting to share their lives.

1967   The "Summer of Love" gave rise to thousands of hippie communes, and also to the first wave of contemporary "egalitarian" communities (including Twin Oaks).

1970s   The FIC database has many hundreds of listings for communities that were started throughout the 1970s—a prolific time for community in the United States.

1972   A Danish architect gathered a group of friends to discuss housing options, which resulted in the creation of a new form of community now called "cohousing."

1986   N-Street, an urban retrofit, was the first cohousing community established in North America. Since then, 42 more have been completed, and 160 communities are in the construction or planning phases (as of fall 1999).

1992   Ecovillages were founded in Ithaca, New York; Los Angeles, California; and St. Petersburg, Russia; marking the start of another new community model.

Reprinted with permission from the Communities Directory, RR 1 Box 156-D, Rutledge, MO 63563, USA, http://directory.ic.org/

Notes

PREFACE

1. *Communities Directory: A Guide to Intentional Communities and Co-operative Living* (Rutlege, MO: Fellowship for Intentional Community, 2000), 15.

2. David Yount, *The Future of Christian Faith in America* (Minneapolis, MN: Augsburg Books, 2003), 10.

3. Quoted in David Martin, "The Shakers: Serene Twilight of a Once Sturdy Sect," *Life* (March 17, 1967): 41.

4. Ibid.

5. Quoted in Flo Morse, *The Shakers and the World's People* (New York: Dodd, Mead), 317.

6. Acts 4: 32.

INTRODUCTION

1. William Wordsworth, "Intimations of Immortality from Recollections of Early Childhood," quoted in John Bartlett, *Familiar Quotations* (Boston: Little, Brown, 1980), 426.

2. Yogi Berra, quoted in Robert Byrne, *The 2,548 Best Things Anybody Ever Said* (New York: Fireside, 2003), 383.

3. Acts 4: 32–35.

4. Rosabeth Moss Kanter, *Commitment and Community: Communes and Utopias in Sociological Perspective* (Cambridge: Harvard University Press, 1972), 56.

5. Charles Nordhoff, *American Utopias* (Stockbridge, MA: Berkshire House, 1993), 19.

6. Kanter, *Commitment and Community,* 75.

7. Ibid., 218.

CHAPTER 1

1. Psalm 133: 1.

2. Gerald Tomlinson, ed. *Treasury of Religious Quotations* (Englewood, NJ: Prentice Hall, 1991), 90.

3. Henry David Thoreau, *Walden* (New Haven, CT: Yale University Press), 90.

4. Matthew 5: 48.

5. Peter Levi, *The Frontiers of Paradise: A Study of Monks and Monasteries* (New York: Weidenfeld & Nicholson, 1990), 1.

6. Ibid., 2.

7. Joel Rippinger, OSB, *The Benedictine Order in the United States: An Interpretive History* (Collegeville, MN: Liturgical Press, 1990), 217.

8. *"Saint Benedict," Butler's Lives of the Saints* (London: Burns & Oates, 1991), 146.

9. Timothy Fry, OSB, ed. *The Rule of St. Benedict* (New York: Vintage, 1998), xvi.

10. Ibid., 3.

11. Ibid., xv.

12. Ibid., xvii.

13. Ibid., xix.

14. Quoted in Tony Augarde, *The Oxford Dictionary of Modern Quotations* (New York: Oxford University Press, 1991), 51.

15. Fry, *Rule of St. Benedict,* 20.

16. Ibid., xxx.

17. Ibid., 27.

18. 1 Thessalonians 5:17.

19. Thomas Moore, *The Soul's Religion* (New York: HarperCollins, 2002), 243.

20. Fry, *Rule of St. Benedict,* 55.

21. Ibid., 33.

22. Tomlinson, *Religious Quotations,* 215.

23. Matthew 25:35.

24. Fry, *Rule of St. Benedict,* 51.

25. Kathleen Norris, *The Cloister Walk* (New York: Riverhead, 1996), 366.

CHAPTER 2

1. John Winthrop, quoted in Daniel Boorstin, *The Americans: The Colonial Experience* (New York: Vintage, 1958), 5.

2. Ibid., 3.

3. Ibid., 3.

4. Ibid.

5. Ibid., 9.

6. Quoted in Perry Miller, ed., *The American Puritans: Their Prose and Poetry* (New York: Doubleday Anchor, 1956), 87.

7. Boorstin, *Americans,* 9.

8. Ibid., 23.

9. Quoted in Bartlett, *Familiar Quotations,* 772.

10. Samuel Eliot Morison, *Builders of the Bay Colony* (Boston: Houghton Mifflin, 1930), 130.

11. Quoted in Perry Miller and Thomas H. Johnson, *The Puritans: A Sourcebook of their Writings,* vol. 2 (New York: Harper & Row, 1963), 512.

12. Bruce C. Daniels, *Puritans at Play: Leisure and Recreation in Colonial New England* (New York: St. Martin's Griffin, 1995), 12.

13. Morison, *Builders,* 131.

14. Quoted in Miller, *Puritans,* 181.

15. Ibid., 91.

16. Daniels, *Puritans at Play,* 110.

17. Ibid., 111.

18. Ibid., 216.

19. Quoted in Morison, *Builders,* 160.

20. Miller, *Puritans,* 172 ff.

21. Ibid.

22. Morison, *Builders,* 43 ff.

23. Ibid., 160.

24. Quoted in Boorstin, *Americans,* 35.

25. Quoted in Morison, *Builders,* 72.

26. Quoted in Boorstin, *Americans,* 30.

27. Quoted in Morison, *Builders,* 368.

28. Miller, *Puritans,* 736.

29. John Putnam Demos, *Entertaining Satan: Witchcraft and the Culture of Early New England* (New York: Oxford University Press, 2004), 201.

30. Quoted in Morison, *Builders,* 47.

31. Demos, *Entertaining Satan,* 202.

32. Quoted in Bartlett, *Familiar Quotations,* 392.

CHAPTER 3

1. Quoted in Boorstin, *Americans*, 33.

2. Rufus M. Jones, *Quakerism: A Spiritual Movement* (Philadelphia: Yearly Meeting of Friends, 1963), 166.

3. Boorstin, *Americans*, 43.

4. Ibid.

5. Ibid., 42.

6. Matthew 6: 34–37.

7. Boorstin, *Americans*, 41.

8. Ibid., 36.

9. Ibid.

10. Ibid., 39.

11. Ruth Plimpton, *Mary Dyer: Biography of a Rebel Quaker* (Boston: Branden Publishing, 1994), 187.

12. Boorstin, *Americans*, 64.

13. Ibid., 64–65.

14. Ibid., 63.

15. Ibid., 51.

16. Ibid., 58.

17. Ibid., 59.

18. Jones, *Quakerism*, 176.

19. Ibid., 175.

20. Boorstin, *Americans*, 307.

21. John Punshon, *Portrait in Grey: A Short History of the Quakers* (London: Quaker Home Service, 1984), 99.

22. Jones, *Quakerism*, 179–80.

CHAPTER 4

1. Donald B. Kraybill, *The Riddle of Amish Culture* (Baltimore: Johns Hopkins University Press, 1989), 24.

2. Ibid., 224.

3. Ibid., 4.

4. Ibid., 29.

5. Ibid.

6. Ibid.

7. Ibid., 30.

8. Ibid., 99–100.

9. Ibid., 100.

10. Ibid., 117.

11. Ibid., 117.

12. Ibid., 192.

13. Ibid., 211.

CHAPTER 5

1. Lawrence Foster, *Women, Family, and Utopia: Communal Experiments of the Shakers, their Oneida Community, and the Mormons* (Syracuse, NY: Syracuse University Press, 1991), 20.

2. Ibid., 23.

3. Flo Morse, *The Shakers and the World's People* (New York: Dodd, Mead, 1991), xi.

4. Nordhoff, *American Utopias*, 144 ff.

5. Ibid., 153.

6. Ibid., 143.

7. Ibid., 167.

8. Ibid., 158.

9. Ibid., 159.

10. Ibid., 160.

11. Ibid., 160–61.

12. Foster, *Communal Experiments*, 30.

13. Ibid., 66.

14. Ibid., 63.

15. Ibid., 68.

16. Morse, *Shakers*, 355.

17. Ibid., 352.

CHAPTER 6

1. James 1: 5.

2. Thomas F. O'Dea, *The Mormons* (Chicago: University of Chicago Press, 1970), 4.

3. Lawrence Wright, "Lives of the Saints," *New Yorker* (January 21, 2002): 47.

4. Ibid.

5. Ibid., 51.

6. Ibid.

7. Ibid., 48.

8. Ibid.

9. William Booth, "An Olympic Challenge: Counter Mormon Image," The *Washington Post* (January 28, 2002): A6.

10. Wright, *New Yorker*, 50.

11. Ibid.

12. Ibid., 44.
13. Ibid., 57.
14. Ibid., 42.
15. Foster, *Communal Experiments*, 202.
16. "The Church of the West," *Economist* (February 16, 2002): 30.
17. Ibid., 29.
18. Ibid., 30.

CHAPTER 7

1. Nordhoff, *American Utopias*, 276.
2. Foster, *Communal Experiments*, 92.
3. Nordhoff, *American Utopias*, 259.
4. Ibid., 265.
5. Ibid.
6. Ibid., 268.
7. Ibid., 269.
8. Ibid., 270.
9. Ibid., 272.
10. Ibid., 275.
11. Ibid., 286.
12. Ibid., 284.
13. Ibid., 281.
14. Ibid., 288.
15. Ibid., 289.
16. Ibid., 292.
17. Ibid., 293.
18. Foster, *Communal Experiments*, 116.
19. Ibid., 108.
20. Ibid., 111.
21. Ibid., 116.
22. Nordhoff, *American Utopias*, 300–301.

CHAPTER 8

1. David Bennett, *William Booth* (Minneapolis, MN: Bethany House), 18.
2. Ibid., 46.
3. Ibid., 25–26.
4. Ibid., 22.
5. Ibid., 24.
6. Ibid.
7. Ibid.

8. Ibid., 119.

9. Edward Bishop, *Blood and Fire: The Story of William Booth and the Salvation Army* (Chicago: Moody Press), 59.

10. Bennett, *William Booth,* 46.

11. Robert A. Watson, and Ben Brown, *The Most Effective Organization in the United States: Leadership Secrets of the Salvation Army* (New York: Crown Business, 2001), 15.

12. Ibid., 16.

13. Ibid., 38.

14. Ibid., 35.

15. Bennett, *William Booth,* 181 ff.

CHAPTER 9

1. *Catholic Worker* (May 2002), 1.

2. Dorothy Day, *On Pilgrimage* (Grand Rapids, MI: Wm. B. Eerdmans, 1999), 42.

3. "I Want to Start a Catholic Worker House," www.catholicworker.org/help/faq.cfm, 8.

4. Tom Cornell, "We Are Still Talking," Sermon delivered on the occasion of the *Catholic Worker's* 69th anniversary, May 1, 2002.

5. Ibid.

6. Robert Ellsberg, "Dorothy Day," Lecture delivered at the New York University Symposium marking the centenary of her birth, November 8, 1997.

7. Mark and Louise Zwick, "Dorothy Day and the Catholic Worker Movement," in *Day,* 10.

8. Dorothy Day, "To Our Readers," *Catholic Worker* (May 1933): 4.

9. Ibid.

10. Dorothy Day, *The Long Loneliness* (New York: Harper & Row, 1952), 195.

11. Ibid., 24.

12. Ibid., 44.

13. Cornell, *Catholic Worker.*

14. *Catholic Worker* (May 2002): 1–3.

15. David Yount, "I Met a Saint in College," unpublished speech on receiving the Knox College Alumni Achievement Award, February 14, 2002.

16. Ellsberg, *Dorothy Day,* 1.

17. Ibid.

18. Ibid.

19. Ibid.

20. Ibid.

21. Robert Coles, *Dorothy Day: A Radical Devotion* (Cambridge, MA: Da Capo Press, 1989), 189.

22. *The Long Loneliness,* iv.
23. Ibid.

CHAPTER 10

1. Genesis 1:25.
2. *Communities Directory: A Guide to Intentional Communities and Co-operative Living* (Rutlege, MO: Fellowship for Intentional Community, 2000), 1.
3. Rosabeth Moss Kanter, *Commitment and Community: Communes and Utopias in Sociological Perspective* (Cambridge, MA: Harvard University Press, 1972), 165.
4. Ibid., 18.
5. Ibid., 237.
6. Ibid., 21.
7. Ibid., 22.
8. Ibid., 25.
9. Markus Baum, *Ebergard Arnold and the Bruderhof* (Farmington, PA: Plough, 1998), 11.
10. Emmy Arnold, *A Joyful Pilgrimage: My Life in Community* (Farmington, PA: Bruderhof Foundation, 2002), 9.
11. Douglas Frantz, and Catherine Collins, *Celebration USA: Living in Disney's Brave New Town* (New York: Henry Holt, 1999), 27.

Bibliography

Andrews, Edward Deming. *The People Called Shakers: A Search for the Perfect Society.* New York: Dover Publications, 1953.

Bennett, David. *William Booth.* Minneapolis, MN: Bethany House, 1986.

Boorstin, Daniel J. *The Americans: The Colonial Experience.* New York: Random House, 1958.

"Saint Benedict," *Joseph Butler Lives of the Saints.* London: Burnes & Oates, 1991.

Carey, John ed. *The Faber Book of Utopias.* London: Faber and Faber, 1999.

Carmody, Denise Lardner, and John Tully Carmody. *The Republic of Many Mansions.* New York: Paragon House, 1990.

Communities Directory: A Guide to Intentional Communities and Cooperative Living. Rutledge, MO: Fellowship for Intentional Community, 2000.

Daniels, Bruce C. *Puritans at Play: Leisure and Recreation in Colonial New England.* New York: St. Martin's Griffin, 1995.

Day, Dorothy. *On Pilgrimage.* Grand Rapids, MI: Eerdmans, 1999.

———. *The Long Loneliness.* New York: Harper and Row, 1952.

Feiss, Hugh, O.S.B. *Essential Monastic Wisdom.* San Francisco: HarperSan-Francisco, 1999.

Fido, Martin, and Keih Skinner. *The Official Encyclopedia of Scotland Yard.* London: Virgin, 2000.

Fishburn, Janet Forsythe. *The Fatherhood of God and the Victorian Family.* Philadelphia: Fortess Press, 1981.

FitzGerald, Frances. *Cities on a Hill: A Journey Through Contemporary American Cultures.* New York: Simon and Schuster, 1986.

Fogarty, Robert S. *American Utopianism.* Itasca, IL: F.E. Peacock Publishers, 1972.

Foster, Lawrence. *Women, Family, and Utopia: Communal Experiments of the Shakers, the Oneida Community, and the Mormons.* Syracuse, NY: Syracuse University Press, 1991.

Fry, Timothy. O.S.B. *The Rule of St. Benedict.* New York: Vintage, 1998.

Furniss, Norman F. *The Mormon Conflict, 1850–1859.* New Haven: Yale University Press, 1960.

Hall, David D. ed. *Puritanism in 17th Century Massachusetts.* New York: Holt Rinehart and Winston, 1968.

Handy, Robert T. ed. *Religion in the American Experience.* New York: Harper and Row, 1972.

Hattersley, Roy. *Blood and Fire: William and Catherine Booth and Their Salvation Army.* New York: Doubleday, 1999.

Kanter, Elizabeth Moss. *Commitment and Community: Communes and Utopias in Sociological Perspective.* Cambridge, MA: Harvard University Press, 1972.

Kateb, George. *Utopia and Its Enemies.* Glencoe, Ill: Free Press, 1963.

Koster, Donald N. *Transcendentalism in America.* Boston: Twayne, 1975.

Kraybill, Donald B. *The Riddle of Amish Culture.* Baltimore: Johns Hopkins University Press, 1989.

McCord, William. *Voyages to Utopia.* New York: W.W. Norton & Company, 1989.

McKinley, Edward H. *Marching to Glory: The History of the Salvation Army in the United States.* San Francisco: Harper and Row, 1980.

Miller, Perry. ed. *The American Puritans: Their Prose and Poetry.* New York: Doubleday Anchor, 1956.

Miller, Perry, and Thomas H. Johnson, eds. *The Puritans.* New York: Harper and Row, 1938.

Morse, Flo. *The Shakers and the World's People.* New York: Dodd, Mead & Company, 1980.

Muelder, Hermann R. *Missionaries and Muckrakers: The First Hundred Years of Knox College.* Urbana: University of Illinois Press, 1984.

Nordhoff, Charles. *American Utopias.* Stockbridge, MA: Berkshire House, 1993.

Norris, Kathleen. *The Cloister Walk.* New York: Riverhead, 1996.

Pool, Daniel. *What Jane Austen Ate and Charles Dickens Knew.* New York: Simon & Schuster, 1993.

Putnam, Robert D. *Bowling Alone: The Collapse and Revival of American Community.* New York: Simon & Schuster, 2000.

Riesman, David. *The Lonely Crowd.* New Haven: Yale University Press, 1950.

———. *Faces in the Crowd.* Nee Haven: Yale University Press, 1952.

Rippinger, Joel. O.S.B. *The Benedictine Order in the United States: An Interpretive History.* Collegeville, MN: The Liturgical Press, 1990.

Robertson, Constance Noyes. *Oneida Community: The Breakup, 1876–1881.* Syracuse, NY: Syracuse University Press, 1972.

Tocqueville, Alexis de. *Democracy in America.* New York: New American Library, 1956.

Utopian Visions. Alexandria, VA: Time-Life Books, 1990.

Waller, George M. *Puritanism in Early America.* Lexington, MA: D.C. Heath and Company, 1973.

Watson, Robert A., and Ben Brown. *The Most Effective Organization in the U.S.* New York: Crown Business, 2001.

Wertenbaker, Thomas Jefferson. *The Puritan Oligarchy.* New York: Grosset's Universal Library, 1947.

———. *The Puritan Oligarchy.* New York: Scribners, 1947.

Anonymous. *What Is Scientology?* Los Angeles: Bridge Publications, 1993.

Index

Adams, Abigail, 27
Addams, Jane (Nobel Peace Prize), 121
agriculture, 54, 63, 86
American democracy, Quaker/Puritan influence of, 22, 41
American Friends Service Committee (Quakers), 41–42
American Revolution, 27, 62
Amish, xv, 43–56; Ammann, Jacob, as founder and, 45; doctrines of, 45, 48; dress of, 45–49; family-fellowship expansion, 43–44; in film, 44; humility and, 45, 52; Kraybill on, 47–51, 53–56; in Lancaster County, Pennsylvania, 43–44, 46; leadership, 51–52; lifestyle, 47–48; as pacifists, 48; social organization/control, 46–52
Anabaptists (rebaptizers), 45. *See also* Amish; Bruderhof; Hutterites
Anthony, Susan B., 42
antislavery, Quaker communities, 30, 39
Arbella (flagship), 16
Armstrong, Eliza, 104
Arnold, Eberhard, 135–37

Bailyn, Bernard, 23
baptism, as adults in Anabaptist/Amish communities, 45–46; 50–51; in Mormon communities, 72, 79, 82
Benedictine monks, 4
Benedict of Nursia (ca. 480–547). *See* Saint Benedict
Bennett, Bob, 81
Bennett, David, 99–102, 105, 111
Berra, Yogi, xiv
birth control, through Oneida perfectionist's "male continence" doctrine, 84
Bloom, Harold, 77
The Book of Mormon (Smith), 72–73, 79
Boorstin, Daniel, 31–32, 34–35, 37, 40
Booth, Ballington (William's son), 107
Booth, Branwell (William's son), 105
Booth, Catherine (William's wife), 114
Booth, Evangeline (William's daughter), 107
Booth, Maud (Ballington's wife), 107
Booth, William, 98–99, 110–11

Boston, MA, 16, 19, 21, 23–25, 30, 35
Boston Latin School, 21
Bradford, William, 15–16
Brigham Young University, 75, 78
Brook Farm (transcendentalist community), xv, xvii
Bruderhof (Place of Brothers) communities, 135–37. *See also* Amish; Anabaptists; Hutterites
Buchanan, James (U.S. President), 74
Burton, Richard, 79
Butler's Lives of Saints, 7

Calvinists. *See* Puritans
Cannon, Chris, 81
The Catholic Worker (newspaper), 114, 117, 119, 121
Catholic Worker Movement, the, xv, xviii; 113–125; cofounder, Dorothy Day, 113, 115–16, 123–4; cofounder, Peter Maurin, 116, 120–21; communities in America, 117–18; Cornell on, 115; Great Depression impact on, 114, 116–17, 121; houses of hospitality, xv, 116–17, 121; humanitarian/peace platform of, 121–23; origins, 116–17; pacifism and, 122–24; publication of, 114, 117, 119, 121–22; Salvation Army *versus,* 114–15
Celebration (Florida) community, 138–39
celibacy, 3, 5, 9, 57–58
charity and social services organization. *See* Salvation Army, the
Charles II (King of England), 33
Charming Nancy (ship), 46
Chaves, Cesar, 115
Chesterson, G. K., 121
children. *See* family; gender roles
Christian communism, Joseph Meacham/Shaker communities, 65–66
Christian Mission (formerly People's Mission Hall), 103

Christian Mission Magazine. See East London Evangelist
Christie Street Catholic Worker (house), 115
Christ's Second Coming, 67
church and state: Mormons and, 80–81; Puritans and, 17, 24–25; Salvation Army, the, and, 108
Church of England, 16
Church of Jesus Christ of Latter-day Saints, 72
The Circular (Communist magazine), 87
"City upon a hill," as John Winthrop's Puritan utopia, 16
Civil War, 62
Cloister, the (monastic communities), 1–13; celibacy and, 5, 9; decline and destruction of monasteries, 6; Divine Office, as daily prayers, 10; hospitality and, 12–13; humility, 8–9; Levi's view of monastic lifestyle, 5; monk's lifestyle, 3–4, 8, 10–11, 12; Norris on, 13; perfectionism as salvation, 9; Saint Benedict's influence on, 6–13; in Utah Trappist communities, 3; wealth's impact on, 5–6; worldwide, "Third Orders," 1
clothing. *See* dress
Coca-Cola (corporation), 76
cohousing, 128, 130
Coleman, Benjamin, 25
Coles, Robert, 125
collectivism. *See specific utopian communities by name.*
Commonwealth of Massachusetts, 21
communion services, 52
communism: of Oneida perfectionists, 86–88
Communist Party, 115
communitarianism and Mormons, 75. *See also* communism of Oneida perfectionists
community activists. *See* Catholic Worker, the

complex marriage, as Oneida doctrine, 84
Conception Abbey, 4
congregationalism, originated by Puritans, 15–18
conscientious objectors to war, 117. *See also* pacifism
Cornell, Tom, 115
Cotton, John, 17
Cowdery, Oliver, 73
Cromwell, Oliver, 6

Dana, Charles, xvii
dancing: amongst the Amish, 50; and Puritans, 21; Daniels on, 21; and Shakers, 59–61, 70; Nordhoff on, 60–61
Daniels, Bruce C., 20, 22
Dark Ages, 3
Day, Dorothy, 113, 115–16, 123–24; Coles on, 125; Ellsberg on, 124–25;
Declaration of Independence, the, 41
Demos, John, 26–27
Deseret (provisional state of the United States), 74
Dewbury, William, 34
Dickens, Charles, 60
Divine Light Principle (Quakers), 31
Divine Office, as daily prayer in cloisters, 10
Divine Truth, 40
divorce, 53, 56, 76
dress: in Amish communities, 45–49; in Salvation Army, 106; in Shaker communities, 65; in Twin Oaks communities, 132
Drucker, Peter, 107
Dyer, Mary, 35–36

East London Evangelist (magazine), 102
East London Mission, 100
economic autonomy. *See* Amish; Shakers
The Economist (magazine), 81–82

ecovillages, 128, 130
education. *See* schools
egalitarianism. *See* gender roles
Ellsberg, Robert, 124
Emerson, Ralph Waldo, 78
Endicott, John, 35
England, 29
Equal Rights Amendment (ERA), 80
eternities (Mormon view), 79
eugenics, experiment in Oneida communities, 84, 93
excommunication, practiced in communities, 12, 17, 46, 52, 80

family: in Amish communities, 43–44, 46–47, 49–56; in Bruderhof communities, 136; in Mormon communities, 71, 75–76, 80; in Oneida communities, 84, 88–91, 93; in Puritan communities, 25; in Salvation Army, the, 104, 118, 121; in Shaker communities, 58, 61–62, 64. *See also* gender roles
farming. *See* agriculture
Fellowship of Intentional Communities (FIC), 127
feminism, 74, 130
"Food for the Millions," Salvation Army shops, 103
foot-washing, symbolical teaching humility and equality, 45, 52
Ford, Harrison, 44
Forty Mile (Hutterite community), 137–38
Foster, Lawrence, 58–60, 66, 80
Fothergill, John, 38–39
Fox, George, 29–30, 32–33, 35, 40
Fraser, Charles, 139
free love, form of at Oneida communities, 75
free will and justification by faith, as Mormon doctrine, 79
Free Will Baptists, 60
French Revolution, 6

Freud, Sigmund, xvi
friendly persuasion, practice of
    Quakers, 36
Friends Committee on National
    Legislation, 42
furniture, made in communities, 55,
    63, 86, 136

Garden of Eden, as in America, 79
gender roles: in Amish communities,
    47–48, 51–52, 55–56; in Hutterite
    communities, 130; in intentional
    communities, 130; in Oneida
    communities, 84–85, 93; in Quaker
    communities, 36, 42; in Salvation
    Army, 109; in Shaker communities,
    56, 58–59, 64, 66
General History of New England
    (Hubbard), 26
Genesis, xiv
Germany (Bruderhof communities),
    136
Gethsemani Abbey, 6
Gibran, Kahlil, 136
Great Awakening, xv
Great Depression, stimulant to the
    Catholic Worker movement, 114,
    116–17, 121
Great Salt Lake (Utah), as home of
    Mormon's "Zion," 71, 74
Growing in Faith (Yount), 59

Hancock Shaker Village
    (Massachusetts), 69
Harmony, 131
Harris, Martin, 73
Harvard, John, 21
Harvard University, 39
Hawthorne, Nathaniel, 19, 26
Heaton, Tim, 75
heaven (Christian view), 13
heaven on earth concept. *See specific
    utopian communities by name;
    utopian communities
    (contemporary)*

Henry VIII, King of England
    (Defender of Faith), 6
Hill, Harry, 106
Hinkley, Gordon B., 78
Holder, Christopher, 34–35
Holton, Harriet A., 85
Holy Cross Abbey, 3–4
Holy Experiment (Penn's), 30, 33–34,
    36, 40, 42
Holy Land, as in America, 79
Holy Spirit, 31, 40, 137
homeless shelters, 77
homosexuality, communities against,
    80
hospitality in communities, xv, 12–13,
    116–17, 121
Hostetler, John, 49
housing, 47–48, 51
*How to Reach the Masses with the
    Gospel* (Booth), 105
Hubbard, William, 26
Hull House, 121
humility, 45, 52
Hutterites, the, xvii, 128, 137–38
hymns: Amish, 51; Salvation
    Army, 97, 108; Shaker, 59, 61,
    64, 70
Indians. *See* Native Americans
intentional communities,
    contemporary, xv, 127–29
inventions, in utopian communities,
    57, 89

Jacobs, Electa, 68
Jacobs, Enoch, 67–68
James I, King of England (James VI,
    King of Scotland), 35
Jefferson, Thomas, 37
Johnson, Sonia, 80
Jones, Rufus, 31, 40, 42

Kanter, Rosabeth Moss, xvi, xvii, 60,
    128, 131–33
Keayne, Robert, 24
Kraybill, Donald B., 47–51, 53–56

labor: in Amish communities, 54–55; gender-neutral in contemporary utopian community, 132
Lamanites, 79
Lancaster County, Pennsylvania. *See* Amish
Lee, Ann, 58, 60
Lee, Shaw, 82
Leonard, John, 130
Levi, Peter, 5
The Liberator (newspaper), 116
London Yearly Meeting, 37–39

masochism, tendency in monastic life, 8
Madison, James, 27
male continence, as Oneida doctrine, 84
manufacturing: in Bruderhof communities, 136; in monastic communities, 10; in Oneida communities, 86. *See also* inventions
Marlborough, 22
marriage, 20, 33, 39, 48, 53, 76. *See also* celibacy; complex marriage; polygamy
The Martyrs Mirror (van Braght), 45
Massachusetts Bay Company, 16
Massachusetts General Court, 16, 35
The Masses (newspaper), 116
Mather, Increase, 21
Maurin, Peter, 116, 120–21
Mayflower compact, 15
McGillis, Kelly, 44
Meacham, Joseph, 60, 65–66
meeting house (Puritans and Quakers), 17, 36
men. *See* gender roles
Mencken, H. L., 19
Mennonites. *See* Amish
Merton, Thomas (Trappist monk), 3–4, 12; influence on American monastery life, 12; *The Seven Story Mountain* (book), 12
Methodist New Connexion, 99

migrant farm workers, 115
Millenial Laws (1845), 67
millennialism. *See* Shakers
Miller, John, 92
Miller, Perry, 26
Miller, William, 67
Millerites (Shakers), 67–69
Momas, George Albert (Elder), 62
monasticism. *See* Cloister, the (monastic communities)
Monk, Peter, 100
Montana, 137–38
Monte Cassino Abbey, 7
Moody, Joshua, 20
Moore, Thomas, 8, 10–11
Mormons (Latter-day Saints), xv, 71–82; Brigham Young and, 71, 74–75; charity and public welfare, 80–81; communistic societies in Ohio/Missouri, 73; doctrines (beliefs) of, 72–73, 78–79; Gentiles *versus*, 82; Joseph Smith, Jr., founder, 72–74, 78–79; lifestyle of, 76–77; Mitt Romney and, 72, 78; origins, 72–74; polygamy of, 74–76, 80; proselytizing and, 77–78; skepticism toward practice of, 82; Tolstoy on Mormonism, 79–80
Moroni, 72–73, 79
Morrison, Samuel Eliot, 19, 26
Mumford, Catherine, 99
Muslims, 105
mutual assistance and separation, Amish doctrine, 48
mutual criticism, as Oneida doctrine, 91

Nauvoo Legion (Illinois militia), 73–74
Nazism, determinant for Bruderhof emigration from Germany, 146
Nephites, 79
New England Puritans, the. *See* Puritans
New Harmony, xv, 131

New Jerusalem, as Mormon empire concept, 71

New Lebanon, 66, 69

New York City, 58, 114, 116–17

nonviolent protesting. *See* Catholic Worker, the

Nordhoff, Charles, xvi, 61–64, 86–92, 91–92, 95

Norris, Kathleen, 13

Noyes, John Humphrey, 83–88, 91–94

Noyes, Pierrepont, 94

Noyes, Theodore, 93

Old Order Amish. *See* Amish

Oneida Community, the, xv, 75, 83–95, 132–33; beliefs, 87–88; *The Circular* (newspaper), 86–87; demise of, 92–94; doctrines, 84, 91; Foster on, 92–94; John H. Noyes, founder (Perfectionists) and, 83–88, 91–94; lifestyle in, 88–90; Nordhoff on, 86–92, 95

Oneida (Twin Oaks building), as symbol for earlier utopia, 130–31

Osmond, Donny, 72

Osmond, Marie, 72

Owen, Robert, 131

pacifism, 32, 36–38; and Catholic Worker, 122–24; and Quakers, 32, 36–38; and Shakers, 62. *See also* Amish; conscientious objectors to war

The Pall Mall Gazette (Stead, W. T.), 104

Paramount Pictures, 44

Peaceable Kingdom (Quakers' utopia), 31

Penn, William, 30, 33–34, 36, 40, 42

Pennsylvania. *See* Quakers

Pennsylvania Dutch Visitor's Bureau, 44

People's Mission Hall, 102

perfectionism, as way of salvation in utopian communities, 85

Perfectionist. *See* Oneida Community, the

Philadelphia, 40, 46

Philadelphia (City of Brotherly Love), 41

Plough Publishing House (Bruderhof enterprise), 137

Plymouth Colony. *See* Puritans

polygamy (plural marriage), Brigham Young and, 74–76; Foster on, 80

priesthood of all believers, as Christian Quaker doctrine, 36

profitable communism, 86–87

prohibition, 107

proselytizing. *See* Mormons; Shakers

Protestant Reformation, 45

Providence (doctrine), 16, 32

Psalms, the. *See* Divine Office, as prayer in cloisters

public confessions, required in Amish communities, 52–53

public welfare, as "faith-based initiative," in Mormon communities, 81

Puritans, xv, 15–27; beliefs/morals of, 15–16, 18–19; Boorstin on, 17; Cotton's ministerial influence on, 17, 24; decline of, 19, 23–24; Demos on, 26–27; John White and, 24; John Winthrop, as founder, 16, 23; lifestyle, 20–21, 22–25; in literature, 19; Morison on, 19–18, 23, 26; pleasures of, 19–20; Daniels on, 19–20; Quakers *versus*, 30–31, 34–36; witches and, 26–27

Quakers (Friends), xv, 29–42; abdication of power, 38–39; beliefs/practice, 29, 31, 36, 41–42; Boorstin on, 31–32, 34–35, 37, 40; characteristics of, 33, 39; Christopher Holder and, 34–35; Dyer, Mary and, 35–36; English influence on, 32–33, 37–39; expansion of, 30, 32–33; founder, George Fox, 29–30, 32–33, 35, 40;

humanitarianism and, 39, 41–42; Jones' on, 31, 40, 42; marginalization of, 33; Native Americans and, 31, 38–39, 41; pacifism and, 32, 36–38; Penn's "Holy Experiment" for tolerance, 30, 33–34, 36, 40, 42; Pennsylvania Assembly and, 32, 37–38; Punshon on, 41; Puritans *versus,* 30–31, 34–36; in United States (current), 33; universal influence, 41
Queen Victoria, 98

Rabbits, Edward, 99
radical utopian planners. *See* Puritans
Rail, George Scott, 105–7
Red Scare, the, 116
Relief Society (Mormon), 80
religious dissenters. *See specific utopian communities by name*
Roaring Twenties, 121
Robertson, Constance Noyes, 94
Roman Catholic Church, 45, 119
Romanus (monk), 7
Romney, Mitt, 72, 78
Ruby, George, 101
Rule of Saint Benedict (the *Rule),* of cenobitic monastic life, 6–13
Russian Revolution, 116

Sudbury (Massachusetts), 22–23
Saint Benedict, 6–13
Salem, Massachusetts, 26
Salt Lake City's Temple Square, 72
Salt Lake Organizing Committee, 72
The Salt Lake Tribune, 82
Salvation Army, the, xviii, 97–111, Bennett on, 99–102, 105, 111; Christian creed (1878), 109; Watson on, 109. Christian mission statement of: Watson on, 107–8; dress of, 106; humanitarianism goals of, 109–10; income from funding/business sources, 103, 108;

locations of, 107; name defined, 97, 105; Railton's role and, 105–7; rules of, 109–10; sex trade of women/children fought by, 104; William Booth, as founder in London, 98–99, 110–11
salvation by personal responsibility, Mormon doctrine, 79
The Salvationist (formerly The Christian Mission magazine), 105
The Scarlet, Letter (Hawthorne), 19
Schneider, Herbert W., 25
schools in: in Amish communities, 46, 49; in monasteries, 28; in Oneida communities, 90; in Puritan communities, 21; in Quaker communities, 39–40
scripture as absolute authority, Amish doctrine, 45
Second Vatican Council, 123
Sermon on the Mount, as Christian tenet for perfect utopian community, 48, 116
The Seven Story Mountain (Merton), 12
sexuality, 75–76, 80, 83–84
Shakers, xv, 57–70; beliefs, 58–62; celibacy and, 66; co-leadership (Meacham/Wright) of, 60, 65–66; dress, 65; Foster on, 58–60, 66; founder, Ann Lee, 58–59, 60, 69; growth increase/decrease of, 63, 66; humanitarianism, 68; Jacobs on, 68; Kanter on, 60; lifestyle, 58–59, 64–65; Millennial Laws (1845) and, 67; Nordhoff on, 61–64; pacifism and, 62; persecution of, 60; as "Shaking Quakers," 59; silence (vs. Quakers), 61. *See also* Quakers
Shaw, George Bernard, 102, 104
Shaw, Lee, 82
shunning, as a practice in Amish communities, 53

Simons, Menno, 45
"Simple Gifts" (hymn), 59
simplicity (plainness). *See* Amish;
    Quakers
Skinner, B. F., 131
Smith, Emma, 73
Smith, Hyrum, 74
Smith, Joseph, Jr., 72–74, 78–79
social service and salvation, as
    Salvation Army quest, 101
Spanish Civil War, 117
spiritual manifestations, in Shaker
    communities, 66–67
spiritual reading (*lectio divina*),
    required in monastic communities,
    11
St. Anselm's Abbey, 3–4
Stead, W. T., 104

temperance movement, 103
"that of God and everyone" (Inner
    light), as Quaker belief, 29
Thoreau, Henry David, 2
Tolstoy, Leo, 79
Townsend, Richard, 31–32
Trappists, as Roman Catholic order,
    3–4
Tribune (Salt Lake City), 80
Trinity, Christian *versus* Mormon
    view, 79
Twin Oaks, 130–34

United Order of Enoch, 73
United Society of Believers in Christ's
    Second Appearing. *See* Shakers
University of Pennsylvania, 39
U.S. Supreme Court, 75
utilitarianism. *See* Shakers
utopian communities (contemporary):
    Freud on, xvi; ideologies of, 129–30;
    Leonard on, 130; overview of, xiii–
    xviii; presence/profiles of, 127–9;
    problems of, 83–84; Twin Oaks,
    as model, 130–34, Kanter on,
    131–33

volunteer services. *See* Salvation Army,
    the
Volunteers of America, 107

Walden Pond (retreat), 2
Walden Two (Skinner, B. F.), 131
Walker, Ronald, W., 78
The War Cry (magazine), 106
Watson, Robert A., 107–8, 109
Westbrook, Emma, 106
Westminster Abbey, 98
White, John, 24
Whitmer, David, 73
Whittaker, James, 69
Wilde, Oscar, 20
Willard, Samuel, 20
William, Bradford, 15–16
William, Roger, 35
William and Mary University, 39
Winthrop, John (Massachusetts
    Governor), 16, 20
witchcraft, 26–27
witchcraft trials, 19, 26
Witness (film), 44
women. *See* gender roles
women's suffrage, 42, 116
The Wonders of the Invisible World
    (Mather), 26
Woodcrest (American Bruderhof
    community), 136
Wordsworth, William, xiii, xvii
workers movement. *See* Catholic
    Worker Movement
Works of Mercy, 120, 122
World War I, 116
World War II, 7, 41, 117
Wright, Lawrence, 76–77

Yale University, 39
Yorkshire mission (Whitby), 104
Young, Brigham, 71

Zion, as Mormon's empire, 71
Zurich City Council, 45
Zwingli, Ulrich, 45

About the Author

DAVID YOUNT, author of 11 previous books, is a columnist with the Scripps Howard News Service. His column *Amazing Grace* is syndicated to 450 newspapers weekly. He has served as vice chairman of the Washington Theological Consortium of Protestant, Catholic, and Islamic seminaries.

Books by David Yount

Growing in Faith
  A Guide for the Reluctant Christian

Breaking through God's Silence
  A Guide to Effective Prayer

Spiritual Simplicity
  Simplify Your Life and Enrich Your Soul

Ten Thoughts to Take into Eternity
  Living Wisely in Light of the Afterlife

Be Strong and Courageous
  Letters to My Children on Being Christian

What Are We to Do?
  Living the Sermon on the Mount

Faith under Fire
  Religion's Role in the American Dream

The Future of Christian Faith in America

Celebrating the Rest of Your Life
  A Baby Boomer's Guide to Spirituality

How the Quakers Invented America

Growing in Faith
  A Guide for the New Millennium